ALSO BY CHERYL RICHARDSON

Take Time for Your Life
Life Makeovers

STAND UP
——for——
YOUR LIFE

A PRACTICAL
STEP-BY-STEP PLAN TO
BUILD INNER CONFIDENCE
AND PERSONAL POWER

Cheryl Richardson

FREE PRESS

New York   London   Toronto   Sydney

FREE PRESS
1230 Avenue of the Americas
New York, New York 10020

The Values List on pages 64–66 is based on the Tru Values Program from
Coach U (www.coachu.com) © 1994. Reprinted with permission.

For information regarding special discounts for bulk purchases,
please contact Simon & Schuster Special Sales at 1-800-456-6798 or
business@simonandschuster.com

Designed by Lisa Chovnick

Manufactured in the United States of America

10   9   8   7   6   5   4   3

The Library of Congress cataloged the hardcover edition as follows:

Richardson, Cheryl
Stand up for your life : a practical step-by-step plan to build inner confidence and personal
power / Cheryl Richardson.
p.   cm.
Includes bibliographical references.
1. Self-actualization (Psychology). I. Title.
BF637.S4.R57   2002
ISBN 0-7432-2650-X
0-7432-2651-8 (Pbk)

To my husband, Michael—the man whose love and support allows me to fulfill my greatest potential.

To my mother, Ann Richardson—the woman who instilled in me a reverence for all life.

To my father, John Richardson—the man who taught me how to bring my work to the world.

I AM BLESSED BEYOND MEASURE to be able to write and publish my work—a privilege that I never take for granted. The amazing people who support my efforts make my ability to help others possible. It is with deep gratitude and appreciation that I thank them here.

I'd first like to thank Marilyn Abraham, the woman who continues to be the guiding force behind my writing. Thank you for your friendship and for inspiring my best work. You continue to be the guardian angel who settles the fear that grips my fingers and I love you dearly.

Michelle Burford helped bring this book to life. Thank you for your dedication, your integrity, and for reminding me about the importance of asking for and receiving help. Your inspiration is on every page.

Ginger Burr is my dear friend who not only helped shape this manuscript, she spent many a night listening to my ideas over and over again. Thank you for your love, your friendship, and for uncurling my fax paper. And a special thank you to Patty Portwine for watching over us both. Fran Massey's editorial comments in the last hour were priceless. Thank you for taking the time out of your busy schedule to make this book better (and a big thanks to Nick Massey for faxing so many pages!). My love and thanks also go to Shirley Anderson, wise woman and coach extraordinaire, for returning me to my spiritual center when I get off track. I love you Yoda.

My literary agent Amanda Urban of ICM is the best in the business. Thank you for your exceptional representation and guidance. Working with you has taught me a lot about standing up for my life. Thanks also to John DeLaney, Helen Shabason, Karen Kenyon, and Margaret Halton for taking care of my literary and television needs—I appreciate your support! And a very special thank you to my attorney Mark Lawless who has been with me from the beginning. You are irreplaceable.

My editor, Dominick Anfuso, is a very special man. Not only is he an exceptional editor, he has a kind heart and a great sense of humor. Thank you for believing in my work and for making the process of publishing such a joy (and for the great laughs!). Thank you also to Carisa Hays for her professionalism and for taking good care of my publicity needs, and to Kristen McGuiness for your support and cheerfulness. Thanks also to Rachel Burd and Carol de Onís for their copyediting expertise. The incorrect grammar is all mine!

I'd like to share my deep appreciation for the men and women at Harpo Productions who worked on the *Lifestyle Makeover Series*. These talented people work extremely hard to bring the best life-changing programs to television. Thank you Katy Murphy Davis for modeling such high standards and a big hug to Jack Mori, Cindy Mori, Stacy Strazis, Danette Kubanda, Andrea Wishom, and Jen Todd Gray—you're the best in the business!

A very special thank you to Oprah Winfrey who continues to raise the bar on what it means to leave a powerful legacy. She's the tough act we all need to follow.

Jan Silva, my right hand, is the kindest and calmest woman I know. Thank you for your commitment and for your love. You make my life sane and I still don't know how I got so lucky to have you. Thank you to my smart and savvy webmaster Laura Franklin, and to my financial whiz Robin Gillette. A big hug and thank you to Heidi Krupp, the publicist whose energy and enthusiasm could light up Manhattan—you're amazing.

Many thanks to the team at Transworld Publishers especially my wonderful editor Brenda Kimber, Larry Finlay, and Helen Edwards. Thanks also to Reid Tracy and Danny Levin for their love and support, and to all the staff at Hay House.

Thanks also go to my TV team at Oxygen—Gerri Laybourne and all the great staff and crew! And special thanks to Linda Corradina and Michelle Hord for your patience and understanding while I finished this book.

Thank you to the folks at my favorite retreat spot—Miraval Life in Balance in Catalina, Arizona. My love and gratitude to Joseph Denucci (one of the wisest men I know), Wyatt Webb, Joe MacDonald, and every member of their incredible staff.

A big thank you to the writers in my life who support my work and my writing process: Joan Borysenko, Terry Real (thanks buddy, for reminding me to enjoy the enchanted space of writing), Andy Carroll, James Van Praagh, Brian Weiss, Joann Davis, Debbie Ford (my self-care sister), Loretta LaRoche, Julie Morgenstern, Alan Clements, and a special thank you to SARK for the writer's packet—it was a soul saver!

Thanks to the people who provided resources and care during my writing process; Jonathan Berg, Gregg at Mad Martha's, Ann Lee for use of Walton's Ocean Front, my friends at Jabberwocky books, Linda Novotny, Ania O'Connor, Alison Shaw, Christine Misiano-Cornelisse, Carol Look, Barry Crites, Lynn McCann, Beth Garland, and a big thank you to the Plum Island Workshop gang who helped me shape the book! Thanks also to Tan Doan and Gam Nguyen for the great food at Viet Grille and to Diane at Nutcracker Bakery for the best chocolate chip peanut cookies in the world!

My heartfelt love and gratitude goes to the dear friends who always stand by me—I love you all; Chris and Greg Barnes, Stacy Brice, Stephen Cluney, Sharon Day, Deirdre DiDonna, Aryn Ekstedt, Rich and Kathy Fettke, Connie Kelley, Bruce Kohl, Nancy Levin, Kelly O'Brien, Ed Shea, Steve Shull, Debbie Stier, Niravi Payne and my dialogue group: Nanna, Helen, Ro, Greta, Ellen and Pat.

To my family: Mom, Dad, Steven, Janice, Donna, Tom, Lisa, Walter, Shelly, Mark, Robert, Karen, Kerri, Missy, Curt and Pat Gerrish. I love you all more than you'll ever know. And to my best friend Max—thanks for keeping me honest, for bringing me chocolate, and for giving me your coat.

To my sweet husband, Michael—the center of my world. I cannot imagine my life without you. Thank you for giving me exactly what I need to do God's work. I love you way more . . .

And finally, I thank God—the Divine force that continues to guide my life.

CONTENTS

Introduction 1

Chapter 1   Who Do You Think You Are? 25

Chapter 2   Define Your Values 63

Chapter 3   Stop Hiding Your Power 79

Chapter 4   Stand Up for Yourself. 117

Chapter 5   Build Your Courage Muscles 151

Chapter 6   Pass Up Good for Great 179

Chapter 7   Center Your Life Around Your Values 195

Chapter 8   Create a Larger Vision for Your Life 221

STAND UP
——for——
YOUR LIFE

Introduction

FOR YEARS I FELT HAUNTED by a persistent inner voice that told me I was meant to do more with my life. Although I earned a good living and enjoyed the company of family and friends, I felt restless and unsatisfied. There was so much I wanted to do with my life but lacked the courage and confidence to take action. At the prompting of a good friend who referred me to her therapist, I finally reached out for help.

As I sat in his office waiting for my first appointment, my eyes stopped at a cartoon hanging on the wall. It was Snoopy, Charlie Brown's dog from the Peanuts comic strip, struggling to balance a doghouse on his back. The caption below the cartoon read: "There's nothing heavier than the burden of potential." As I stared at that message I started to cry. I too felt burdened by my unrealized potential. I was bursting with energy and desire but lacked the skills to channel it in the right direction.

Once I realized that I could release this burden by taking specific actions to build my confidence and self esteem I got to work. Using the gift of guidance and a whole new action plan, I set about making the changes that allowed my true self to emerge. With each tough choice and courageous step I slowly

1

learned to trust and act on the wisdom of my inner voice. As I did, my life began to change in ways I never would have imagined. Yours can too. In this book I'll offer you a step-by-step plan to unlock and use your greatest potential. As you do, you'll not only give birth to an amazing life, you'll be given an opportunity to help others do the same. To begin, you need only consider the possibilities . . .

What would your life be like if you had the courage and emotional strength to overcome self-doubt, fear, or concern for what others say about you? Think about it. How would your relationships change? Would you stay at your current job? Are there any big moves you'd feel liberated to make? How would your life be different?

From my work with thousands of people, I know that many feel as though they're living a life scripted or prescribed by others. They long to break out of their self-imposed limitations and lead their own lives, but they lack the courage and confidence to do so. The situations are varied. For example, one client who had a successful career in health care said: "I'm dying to start my own restaurant, but I'm afraid of disappointing my father by leaving the family business." Another told me: "Every day I fantasize about traveling throughout Europe, but I keep putting off my plans because I'm too afraid to step outside of my comfort zone." And one mom, echoing the longings of many, said, "I know that my child's welfare comes first, but I can't help feeling that there's something more I'm meant to do with my life."

I understand these yearnings. For years I let fear and self-doubt rule my life, too afraid to step out on my own and follow my true desires. I designed my life according to the blueprints of others. I made people-pleasing a full-time career, trusted the advice of friends before my own, and sabotaged my success each time I came too close to doing something other than what others thought I should do. It wasn't until I faced the truth of how attached I was to the opinions of everyone else that I realized how clueless I was about my own.

If you feel as though your life revolves around the needs or expectations of others, here's an important message for you to hear:

You have deep within you the power to fulfill your highest vision of your life. To engage this power you must develop a solid personal relationship with yourself. By doing so, you'll tap into a wealth of inner strength that will allow you to take the necessary actions that build confidence and self-esteem. When you learn to stop hiding your power and use fear to your advantage, you'll become less attached to what others want for you and more attached to what you want for yourself. As this shift occurs, you'll naturally begin to lead a more authentic and passionate life.

Where do you begin when you decide to stand up for your life? The first step is to develop self awareness. How you handle your day-to-day reality holds clues to the ways you deny your feelings and needs, weaken your emotional strength, and allow others to direct your life. To see what I mean, read through the following list and put a check mark next to the statements that are true for you:

_____ I have responsibilities that prevent me from doing what I really want.

_____ Though I schedule time for myself, I often end up canceling it to accommodate someone else's needs.

_____ I tend to care too much about what others think of me.

_____ Each time I get close to success, I do something to sabotage my progress.

_____ When faced with any decision, I immediately call several people for input.

_____ When someone hurts my feelings, I keep my mouth shut and later fantasize about what I could have said.

_____ I often say yes when I mean no.

_____ I take things personally and feel easily affected by others.

_____ I feel like I'm not living up to my fullest potential.

_____ When speaking with others, I often downplay my knowledge to avoid seeming arrogant.

_____ I'm afraid to out-succeed my parents.

_____ I have a nagging sense that something is missing from my life.

_____ When I'm upset with someone I'd rather talk myself out of it than confront the person with the issue.

_____ I have a secret desire that I've never admitted to anyone.

_____ When someone neglects to follow through on a promise, I quietly brood and do it myself.

_____ I long to find my passion or purpose in life.

If you've checked off even one of these statements, read on . . .

Over the last several years I've listened closely to the needs of my readers. By talking with them during live workshops, communicating electronically with my on-line community, conducting teleconferencing discussions, and leading the Lifestyle Makeover series for the Oprah Winfrey Show, I've met men and women from all walks of life. I've seen the epidemic of frustration and despair.

Parents, homemakers, corporate employees, business owners, artists, and students alike all struggle with the same questions:

- How do I learn to speak up and honor my needs without feeling selfish?

- Where do I find the courage to make the changes I know I need to make in spite of the reactions of others?

- How can I overcome the self-defeating behaviors that make me feel stuck?

- Is there a way to set boundaries without damaging my relationships or feeling guilty?

- How can I stay motivated and stop sabotaging my success?

- How do I find my life purpose—some kind of meaning or direction for my life?

These questions represent the inner challenges we all face as we attempt to find satisfaction in our lives. In my first two books, *Take Time for Your Life* and *Life Makeovers*, I offered practical strategies that allowed readers to begin reclaiming their lives. By practicing the basics of good self-care and tackling those areas that were causing the most stress—cluttered environments, poor financial health, or nonstop, draining to-do lists—many of you joined me in a plan to take more control of your lives. As you set about making these *outer* changes you may have bumped up against *inner* changes that needed to be made as well. For example, you may have wanted a way to deal with your guilty feelings as you made your needs more of a priority. Or you may have needed a strategy to handle your fear as you took bold steps to pursue a lifelong dream. Maybe you felt incapable of handling the inevitable conflict that would occur as a result of making a decision to take control of your life.

ARE YOU GIVING UP YOUR POWER?

When you decide to improve the quality of your life you set in motion new relationships with yourself and others. As you start to take better care of yourself there's a good chance that you'll feel uncomfortable at first, and that some of the people in your life will feel threatened. For example, if you've always said "yes" to family members who need your help, when you start saying "no" it will ruffle some feathers. If you're used to putting the needs of your children before your own, you will feel guilty when you start to make your needs more of a priority. When these reactions to your newfound commitment to self-care occur there's a good chance that you'll do what most caring people do—back down to avoid conflict, hurting others' feelings, disapproval, or abandonment.

Most of us play it safe by putting our needs aside when faced with the possibility of feeling guilty, disappointing others, or facing conflict of some kind. At home you may abdicate your need for support with the kids to keep peace with your spouse, letting your resentment build over time. At work you may allow a complaining coworker to keep draining your energy to avoid confrontation—and end up hating your job. Or you may go right back to saying yes to family members who give you a hard time to avoid their emotional rejection, only to feel frustrated by the lack of quality time that you have for yourself. We work hard to manage the perceptions of others, ignoring our own needs, and in the end we surrender the very thing that will allow us to live authentic, meaningful lives—our power.

We have been trained to surrender our power early in life. Each of us has been taught to live by the rules imposed on us in both subtle and not so subtle ways by generations of parental influences, societal demands, religious expectations, and educational training. Maybe you'll recognize a few of these rules:

> Be nice.
>
> Be quiet.
>
> Don't get too excited.
>
> Don't get too big for your britches.
>
> Be seen and not heard.
>
> Put the needs of others before your own.
>
> Keep your expectations low.
>
> Be modest.
>
> Keep peace at any cost.
>
> Don't out-succeed your loved ones.
>
> Don't threaten others by being too bright.
>
> Don't toot your own horn.
>
> Do what I tell you to do.
>
> Don't be too proud of yourself.
>
> Be happy with what you have.
>
> Don't be a know-it-all.
>
> Don't be so full of yourself.

Although the intention is to use these rules in a constructive, healthy way, more often than not, little by little, they end up stifling a child's spirit. I once witnessed a startling example of this while fishing with a friend who was 79 years old. A young boy approached us and offered to help me cast my rod farther out. He said he was an excellent fisherman, well trained by his grandfather, and added with a proud voice: "I'm pretty smart when it comes to catching fish." No sooner were the words out of this boy's mouth when my friend piped up and said, "Yeah, and you're pretty modest too!"

Instantly I felt the emotional hit in my body and turned just in time to see the young boy shut down too. He dropped his head and started to walk away. My friend meant no harm by his comment; it simply reflected the rule he had been taught to follow: Don't be boastful.

By teaching our children to stay in line we create well-behaved *followers*. While this may make parenting a bit easier, it has enormous costs later in life: These same children grow up to be unhappy adults who desperately want to *lead* their own lives, yet lack the necessary skills to do so.

Instead of being trained to follow the rules that may have crushed your spirit, imagine what your life would have been like if you had been taught these instead:

Stop apologizing when you've done nothing wrong.

Be courageous.

Think big.

Be ambitious.

Don't be modest.

Be seen *and* heard.

Be enthusiastic.

Be proud of who you are and what you know.

Keep your expectations high.

Go for it!

When I think about how my life might have been different had I been raised with these types of rules, I know I would have spoken up in school when I knew the answer to a teacher's question instead of feeling too insecure to raise my hand. I would have performed in the high school plays that captured my imagination rather than relegating myself to the audience secretly longing to be on stage. And as I grew older I would have had the courage to leave the relationships that wounded my heart instead of sticking around, desperately trying to be "good enough." I wonder what you would have done differently? Would you have taken more risks, allowed yourself to stand out from the crowd, or used your talents instead of keeping them hidden?

WHO DO YOU THINK YOU ARE?

Owning our talents and gifts can feel like a risky proposition. When we speak up for what we want and take the actions to make it happen, others may react in a hurtful way. For example, your best friend may get snippy as your new job makes you less available. Or your mother might become emotionally distant when your happy marriage reminds her of what's missing in her own relationship. As we start to out-succeed our loved ones our discomfort with success heightens. We become a target when we have something others want. Rather than rocking the boat and being faced with hearing the question "Who do you think you are?" we settle into a semicomfortable relationship with dissatisfaction. It's much safer to be needy.

We offer each other far more support for suffering than success. Success threatens. When you accomplish great things you tap into the unhealed wounds of those around you and remind them of their own lost dreams or unmet needs. A woman in one of my audiences said it well:

When my husband left me for a younger woman, my friends instantly rallied to support me during my divorce. They came to my rescue, made meals, and talked with me late into the night. Two years later, when I had recovered emotionally, lost 30 pounds, and received a big promotion at work, these same friends began gossiping behind my back about how "full of myself" I'd become. I had changed. I was stronger, more confident, and a lot less needy. I guess they couldn't handle it, but that didn't make the hurt any less painful.

It can be a confusing and tense time as we struggle with the emotions that erupt around another's success. How do we deal with the complicated feelings of envy and joy or the fear of being left behind? I can still remember the discomfort I felt as I watched my friends achieve the kind of goals I wanted for myself. On one hand I felt happy for their accomplishments, and on the other, jealous of their success. I felt confused and embarrassed by these feelings. Over time I learned to see them as an indication that I needed to grow in some way. For example, I began to understand that my jealousy was a signal that there was some action *I* needed to take to move my own career forward. My fear revealed a belief that there wasn't enough success to go around. As I worked through these issues and followed the journey that I'll now share with you, I ignited my passion, and my career began to take off. Soon I found myself on the other side of the equation.

As I started earning more money and achieving the success I desired, I felt uncomfortable talking about it in the company of some friends. Up until that point, so many of our conversations revolved around what wasn't working in our lives, and suddenly I didn't have a lot to say. I knew how to talk about my dissatisfaction, but I had no experience in talking about my success. I was afraid that sharing my accomplishments might appear boastful or spark feelings of jealousy and competition (the same feelings I'd felt before). So I let others do the talking. And when I felt really uncomfortable, I even found myself looking for what wasn't working just to level the playing field.

How you choose to respond to the reactions of others has serious consequences. When my client Kate decided to make her needs more of a priority, she asked her husband to take on more responsibility at home. The mother of two small children, Kate worked full time and handled most of the household chores. After complaining about the inequality at home and getting the cold shoulder from her husband, Kate made the decision to keep silent. Instead of causing a fight by challenging her husband's response, she acquiesced and continued to manage their home. But over time her choice to remain silent had enormous costs. She became increasingly irritable with her children, her neck grew tight, and her back hurt constantly, and little by little her growing resentment whittled away at the intimacy in her marriage.

Another client, Carol, a medical researcher for a biotech company, was considered one of the best problem-solvers in the organization. Whenever her colleague Michael got stuck with a project, he took advantage of her reputation by turning to her for advice and taking credit for the result. Over the years Carol had simply ignored his need to take ownership of her ideas, but this time, after coming up with a successful new way to test a drug and sharing it with Michael, she was furious at him for suggesting to management that he had discovered the procedure. Though Carol wanted to confront this act of betrayal, she lacked the courage to do so. When she came to me for help in finding a new job, she soon realized that she needed to find her courage first. If Carol ran from this situation without learning to speak up for herself, the problem would only follow her to the next position.

Sometimes, the way in which we give up our lives to others takes a different form. Rather than keep silent or make choices in reaction to our fear, we hold ourselves back from the success we deserve by sabotaging our efforts. My friend Chris is a good example.

Chris had a masters' degree in finance and, through hard work, had captured a terrific job in the private banking industry. As his income and professional status grew, his anxiety quickly followed. Chris noticed that family members had started making snide remarks about his upgraded lifestyle. During one family dinner in particular, Chris's mother made a sarcastic comment about the flashiness of his new car. It was shortly after that that Chris told me that his work habits were shifting. He didn't feel as excited as he once had and felt he was losing his edge. Chris started showing up late for work and even missed a couple of important meetings. He began to question whether the career he had chosen was right for him. When I suggested that his lack of motivation might have something to do with his family's reaction to his success, he admitted that he felt guilty about out-succeeding them. His lax behavior at work was his unconscious way of sabotaging his success.

When we ignore our feelings and allow others to rob us of self-esteem, or hide our greatest assets out of a fear of becoming the target of another's jealousy, we commit an act of self-betrayal that has grave consequences. Each act of self-betrayal may keep the boat safely in balance for the moment, but they will severely diminish our self-esteem over time. Ironically, as our sense of self diminishes, we become even more reliant on what others think. As this vicious cycle continues to play out, we slowly lose our passion and desire for life. Filled with doubt and resentment, we eventually face the stark realization that we are living everyone else's life but our own.

There are several behaviors that prevent most of us from leading our own lives. See if you identify with any of the following:

- You feel disconnected from yourself. The quality of your life has been compromised by your ability to do more and feel less. You've lost touch with the very things you need to experience a meaningful life: a strong connection to your feelings and an ability to act on their wisdom.

- You long to experience a sense of fulfillment and purpose but you've centered your life around "shoulds" instead of what you value most.

- You hide your power. You put yourself down or minimize your strengths and talents by engaging in self-defeating behaviors that weaken your self-esteem.

- You care too much about what others think. You work hard at managing the perceptions of others to avoid confrontation and feelings of guilt. You allow people to rob you of time, energy, and self-esteem.

- You allow fear to prevent you from making the changes you really want to make in your life.

- You settle for less than you deserve. Your desire for instant gratification prevents you from making choices that are in your highest interest.

- You long to realize your full potential but you stay put because you don't know where to begin.

- Your belief that abundance is limited prevents you from supporting the accomplishments of others. You've learned to bond with others through suffering instead of success.

These behaviors are in place for a reason. When you begin to relinquish your "follower" role, you may feel disoriented and afraid. There's a good chance that you'll feel confused about your direction in life. When you stand up for your life, you risk the loss of emotional closeness and camaraderie that you may have shared with family, friends, and colleagues, and this connection is important. The need to belong is hard-wired into our brains. When you develop the confidence and inner security to live your own life, this basic need is threatened. Loved ones, fearing abandonment, may attempt to hold you back by reminding you of the potential pitfalls in your plan. Perhaps colleagues who feel frustrated with their own lack of advancement might make snide remarks behind your back as you move up the ladder at work. When you take the leap you have no way of knowing that in reality, as you honor your needs, your true relationships will deepen and new people will come into your life to replace those you may outgrow.

STAND UP FOR YOUR LIFE

In this book I'll take you on a journey that will provide you with new "self-honoring" strategies to transform your fear and self-doubt into power. You'll learn to develop self-trust. You'll build new courage muscles that will increase your self-esteem. And you'll develop the confidence to step out into unknown territory so you can realize your greatest potential. As you learn to stand up for your life, you'll begin to live a life of integrity—a life that makes a powerful contribution to others.

As you work through the program in this book, I'll challenge you to:

- *Know who you are*—build such a strong relationship with yourself that you'll stop taking things personally and start making choices based on what *you* want instead of what others want for you—and you won't think it's selfish.

- *Define your values*—identify your values and the ways in which you and your life need to change in order to center your life around these values.

- *Stop hiding your power*—uncover the ways in which you hide your power and eliminate those self-defeating behaviors that chip away at your self-esteem and prevent you from using your full talents and gifts.

- *Stand up for yourself*—acquire the necessary skills and language to speak up for what you want and say no firmly and gracefully to what you don't want. By facing your fear of conflict head on, you'll discover one of the best ways to build emotional strength—the kind of strength that will serve you in all areas of your life.

- *Build your courage muscles*—use fear as your ally by taking more risks and expanding your comfort zone, so you can make the life changes that really matter.

- *Pass up good for great*—identify and honor your spiritual standards so you can make wise choices for yourself and your life by learning to pass up good for great.

- *Center your life around your values*—take action to make the changes that will center your life around your values.

- *Create a larger vision for your life*—share your success with others by committing your life to being of service and by passing on these skills to loved ones, especially children.

This journey won't be easy. By following this path you'll be making a decision to rock the boat. As you do the exercises and apply the advice to your life, you'll be sending a message to the universe that you're ready to challenge your self-doubt and fear of what others think. And believe me, when you make this proclamation, the universe will respond. You'll be sent the exact people and circumstances you'll need to develop the kind of "inner security" that no bank account, relationship, or job can ever give you.

The truth is this: There is no other way to live the kind of life you long for—one that reflects your deepest desires and allows you to use your greatest gifts—the gifts you've come here to share with the world.

Pretty soon, you'll hear yourself saying:

I know who I am.

I know what I value.

I express my power.

I tell the truth (even when it's uncomfortable) and face conflict with grace and confidence.

I use fear to my advantage.

I trust myself to make choices that honor my highest good.

I live a life centered around my values.

I support and celebrate the accomplishments of others.

If you're ready to stand up for your life, you've picked up the right book. Before we get started, there's one more important thing you need to know—your secret to success.

THE SECRET TO SUCCESS—YOUR CIRCLE OF SUPPORT

The thousands of people who have already joined with others to do the programs outlined in *Take Time for Your Life* and *Life Makeovers* could let you in on a secret: The key to long-lasting motivation and change lies in creating a circle of support. As you take the steps outlined in this book you'll need to surround yourself with others who encourage your choice for change.

Standing up for your life will require you to take courageous steps, and a community of supportive people who are committed to their own growth will become your emotional rock—the solid foundation to stand upon until you can stand firmly on your own two feet.

After listening to the success stories of thousands of people over the years, I've seen the dramatic difference support has made for so many. A high percentage of those who use the power of partnership succeed in making changes that dramatically improve the quality of their lives. After all, it's much easier to confront a problem in your marriage or to ask for a long overdue raise when you know you have a safety net beneath you. There is power in community.

Along with providing the courage to face change, there are other benefits to creating a supportive community for yourself. With smart group guidelines in place that prevent gossip and complaining, you'll learn to bond with others through success instead of suffering. You'll experience the richness of moving beyond surface-level chitchat to more intimate conversations. And you'll make long-lasting friendships that will add more depth and meaning to your life than any material possession ever could.

While you might decide to do this work on your own (which is perfectly fine), consider sharing some of your progress with a trusted family member or friend. Celebrate your success and ask for assistance when you get stuck. When I refer to using your partner or Life Makeover Group for support throughout the program, this may be a good time for you to stop and consider whether or not you could use some extra help.

As you move forward on your spiritual journey, you deserve

to have the support of others who will help keep you on track. You probably already know people who are or should be in your circle—four or five friends or family members you can trust to support you in making the changes that will make a difference. To find out who's qualified to be in your circle, answer the following questions:

- Who are the people who stand in your corner during your most difficult moments?

- Which friends have risked telling you the hard truth with grace and love, simply because they care about you?

- Which of your friends refuses to belittle or tear down others, even when those people are not around?

- Who holds you accountable for what you say you're going to do?

- With whom do you feel absolutely safe?

Your answers to these questions may reveal some of the people who would fit nicely into your circle of support, but if you come up short (which most people do), take heart. I'll not only show you how to create your own circle of support, I'll help you connect with others who are looking for someone just like you.

Take Action! Start a Life Makeover Group

Wouldn't you love an opportunity to meet with a small group of people who are just as anxious and ready for change in their lives as you are? Using my website as a central location, I've created a place for people to find each other. The goal is to offer any individual who is ready to make changes the access to free, in-person meetings that provide mutual positive support. In January 2001, using my existing on-line community—the Life Makeover Community—I decided to start *Life Makeover Groups* around the world. These groups are designed to be a safe place where people can get the support they need to make the changes they've always wanted to make.

Visit us at *www.cherylrichardson.com,* where you'll find everything you need to start and run a successful Life Makeover Group. You'll learn how to profile an ideal member, find new members to join you, locate places where you can hold your group meetings, and the best guidelines for how to run a successful meeting. If you'd rather join an existing group, we have an on-line database of open groups in search of new members. If you don't own a computer, simply visit your local library, log on to their computer, and print out the information you need.

I've learned a lot about what makes for a successful group experience. Members who take their participation seriously and do what it takes to get their needs met have the most success. Some members prefer to form groups with people who share certain lifestyle issues or situations—moms with small children, business owners, or empty nesters. Others prefer to be part of a more diverse group. The size of the group is important too. Experience has shown that the most productive and effective groups have no more than 6 or 8 members.

Since the intention is to create community and to stay in action, it's important for your group to meet regularly. Weekly is best, biweekly is next to best, and monthly works well when you buddy up with someone you can check in with by phone every week. Commitment is the key to success. If you decide to start a group, have members make a commitment to attend for at least three months, and schedule these meetings in advance to make planning easy and to demonstrate *your* commitment to the group.

Let's review the guidelines for the best way to use this book and have a successful group experience:

- Review the entire book before doing the program.

- Choose a person (or persons) you can trust, and be sure that they are committed to the process of completing this book.

- Pick a regular time to meet (at least once a month) either in person or over the phone.

- Read one chapter (or section) at a time before getting together.

Once you're together you can use the following format to make these meetings productive and supportive:

- Start the meeting by sharing your success. What did you learn about yourself? What action steps have you taken? Give each person a chance to brag!

- Spend time discussing the material that you've read in preparation for this meeting. Talk about your experience doing the exercises.

- Decide on the specific actions that you'll each take before your next meeting.

- Ask for help. Use the last fifteen minutes of the meeting to request any support you might need—a check-in phone call, a special resource, or a helping hand.

As you set out to do the exercises in this book, please remember the following:

- Buy yourself a journal or notebook to use in conjunction with this book.

- Each time you see the words *Take Action!* use this as a sign to take action immediately. Small steps make a big difference!

- Take your time doing the exercises and enjoy the process. If you feel overwhelmed by strong emotions, reach out to your group members for support. You might also seek the guidance of a good therapist (you'll find more information about this on pages 57–58 in chapter one). You deserve to have great emotional support in place as you reclaim your power.

- Celebrate your success! Don't wait to complete the book (or a chapter) before you do something special to acknowledge your progress. Reward is the best motivation of all. As you complete an exercise, you might schedule dinner with a good friend, buy yourself a small gift, or enjoy some down time.

For more information about how to facilitate a successful Life Makeover Group, see the guidelines starting on the opposite page.

Whether you've created your circle of support or have decided to go through the program on your own, you're ready for the first step. Let's get started!

———

FOLLOW SMART GROUP GUIDELINES

The following guidelines not only help create a safe place for a productive and enjoyable meeting, they help to eliminate the kind of habits that quickly dissolve a group. I recommend that you review the following guidelines at the beginning of every meeting:

- **Commit to Confidentiality.** Everything that is said at a Life Makeover Group meeting is strictly confidential.

- **Give Everyone Equal Time.** Be sure that each person has a chance to speak. While there may certainly be times when a member needs extra attention, it's important to prevent members from continuously dominating the conversation. This is the one problem that I've seen ruin a group quicker than any other. To ensure that everyone gets equal time, use a timer or an alarm clock to keep members on track. Make sure that it sounds an alarm when time is up. Remember that your meeting should be focused on action, not social chitchat.

- **Don't be critical or give unsolicited advice.** Let each person ask for what they need.

- **Share Facilitation.** Have someone new facilitate your meetings each time you meet to prevent the group from having a "boss." This is also important for those members who have a tendency to get caught up in the "teacher" role and end up not getting the support they need. Too often a member who needs the most support is the one who will take on the caretaker role of the group. Avoid this tendency by rotating leadership.

- **Focus on the positive.** Put the attention on what works. Look for and acknowledge a member's strengths. Keep complaining and whining to a minimum—one minute or less. (We all need to do it sometimes.) If someone continuously comes to a meeting complaining or crying about the same problem without taking action to remedy the situation, this may be an indication that the member needs therapy or some other kind of individual support. Do this member a favor and be honest. Have someone from the group contact the person privately and offer to help them get the support they need. Don't let a fellow member suffer by being "nice." Tell the truth.

- **Speak from your own experience.** Use the word "I" not "you" when speaking to other members.

- **Honor the group.** Hold a regular "check-in" meeting to be sure that all members are satisfied with how the meetings are run. Tell the truth about how you feel (gracefully, of course). You might also check in at the end of each meeting, once a month, or once a quarter. If there is a problem, address it immediately! For example, if someone talks too much or ignores group guidelines by gossiping, you need to honor your group by telling the truth.

CHAPTER ONE

Who Do You Think You Are?

M Y FRIEND MONIQUE called me shortly after September 11, 2001. She said she was finally ready to take her life seriously. She admitted: "For years I've wanted to study acting and I haven't done a thing about it. I've been too afraid of dealing with the fallout from my family and friends. Three years ago when I mentioned my dream to my brother, he teased me relentlessly about wanting to be a star. So I pushed that dream down deep and have remained a 'good girl' ever since. I know I have talent and something important to share with the world and I refuse to hide that part of me any longer. Although I'm afraid that I might not have what it takes, I'm tired of letting my fear hold me back. I'm no longer willing to live with this nagging feeling that there is someone inside of me, someone powerful and determined, who is dying to get out. I want her out and I want my life to mean something."

Monique's declaration to start leading her own life was a courageous step in the right direction. Shortly after our conversation she enrolled in an acting class and decided to face her fear of how others might respond by setting up a meeting with two close friends. Monique explained that her dream of acting was deeply important to her and that she wanted their support. She was surprised to find that both friends were fully on board.

Monique's self-doubt and fear are normal. When you decide to stretch beyond your familiar comfort zone and behave in new, more empowered ways, there's a good chance that you'll mentally look over your shoulder expecting to hear: "Who do you think you are?" Challenging the rules that told you to stay in line or to not get too big for your britches, means exposing yourself to criticism, judgment, and the opinions of others. It is this fear of being exposed that lies at the core of what holds us back from standing in the fullness of who we are.

I understand this fear well. For more than 15 years I had helped people design and follow plans to improve the quality of their lives. After several years of speaking around the country, I finally mustered the courage to pursue my calling to write my first book, *Take Time for Your Life*. As soon as I made the decision to get started a little voice began to pull me back into line with questions like: "Who do you think you are to even consider writing a book? What makes you think you have something important to say?" Immediately I felt vulnerable and afraid. Could I handle being criticized or rejected? Did I have the emotional strength to step into the spotlight and subject myself to the scrutiny of others?

These were the same questions I had heard my clients ask for years. Bright and talented men and women privately would share their fear of how they might be judged by others if they pursued their own independent goals and dreams. These vulnerable feelings caused them to question their talents and the validity of what they had to offer. It always came back to the same old fear: worrying about what others would think. Like me, they had been well trained to suppress their deepest desires for the approval of others. Fortunately, with courage and a commitment to personal and spiritual growth, the soul always wins.

In January 1999, when my book was released, I was excited and optimistic. I was also edgy and nervous. There were many times throughout the process when I was tempted to give in to the critical voices in my head that told me to play it safe. And of course there were the critical external voices as well—a mean-spirited review or e-mail from someone who felt that I needed to conduct my life by their standards instead of my own. In the beginning the opinions of others caused me a tremendous amount of suffering. I learned quickly, however, that a stronger attachment to my inner life as well as a commitment to serve others, were the keys to quieting these fears and finding the inner security and peace that I needed to continue with my plan.

You will always be afraid of hearing the question "Who do you think you are?" until you are able to answer that question for yourself. When you decide to make your personal and spiritual development a top priority by creating a rock-solid relationship with yourself, you gain the power and confidence to make your greatest contribution to the world. You stop caring so much about what others think and start caring more about who you are becoming and how you will make a difference in the lives of others. You shift from being self-involved to confident, courageous, and emotionally strong—the exact qualities you'll need to lead a purposeful life that means something.

YOUR LIFE PURPOSE

For years I've traveled around the country speaking with people about the quality of their lives. If there is one question I am asked over and over again, it's this one: "How can I discover my life purpose and make a difference in the world?" When I hear this question I know it usually means two things. First, the person asking the question is probably unhappy with his or her current circumstances. Second, their soul, the very essence of who they are, yearns to be expressed in their life more fully.

We all want to make a difference in the world. We want to know that our lives matter, that our presence on Earth has meaning and purpose. When I'm asked by clients to help them figure out their purpose for being here I offer the following reply: Each one of us has a Divine assignment—an important mission to fulfill. This assignment consists of two parts. First, you must make your personal and spiritual development a top priority by following your own unique path toward healing and growth. Second, as you develop a strong character by doing this work, you are also charged with improving the world in some way.

There is a reason why your personal work comes first. When you make a conscious commitment to your own inner development, you take a giant step toward making a greater contribution to others. Though it seems at first glance to be selfish to focus on your own life, when you realize that we are all connected by a greater power at work in the world, you begin to understand how fulfilling your individual assignment directly benefits others. As you focus on strengthening your integrity and character you make your greatest contribution to humanity.

History books are filled with individuals who caused change in the world as a result of their own personal work. For example, Bill Wilson, the founder of Alcoholics Anonymous, a man whose legacy has saved millions, made this contribution as a result of his own healing and spiritual development. On a more personal level, I've seen friends and family members do the same thing. My friend Connie, a liver transplant recipient, went on to create an international newsletter that offered hope to thousands of people around the world who were waiting for a life-saving organ. Her willingness to use her own life crisis as a spiritual springboard that strengthened her understanding of herself as a powerful being, allowed her to make a profound difference in the world. You can too.

The first step toward fulfilling your Divine assignment is to take a leadership role in your life. Accepting this role means relinquishing the "follower" position that so many of us have found comfortable and safe. You must become the leader of your own life.

WHO ARE YOU?

The program I've outlined in this book is designed to help you answer the question "Who are you?" By taking specific actions to reclaim your power and build your confidence, you will fulfill your Divine assignment. This program won't be easy. You will face your own internal and external critics. But with hard work and a solid commitment to yourself, you'll know exactly what it feels like to stand in the fullness of who you are.

Becoming the Artist of Your Life

We are all here for a very short, indeterminate amount of time. It's imperative that we use this time well by making our spiritual development a top priority. As you do, I can assure you that you will begin to understand and fulfill your unique purpose here on Earth. This commitment takes time, energy, and a willingness to open your heart and your mind to change. The first step is to realize that *you* are the force for change in your life. No one else can set your destiny, settle your grievances, heal your wounds, or tell you what to do. *You must take full responsibility for an amazing gift that was bestowed upon you at birth—the power to create your life as a work of art.*

Life is far too precious to let anything get in the way of achieving your highest vision—the Divine assignment you've come here to fulfill. You are an artist. The canvas is your life. From this moment on, by accepting this fact, you set in motion the creation of your life as a work of art. To embrace this gift you must be willing to take complete responsibility for all that occurs in your life from this day forward.

There can be great power, as well as great peace, in taking ownership of your life. As you do, you'll begin to see that every person, circumstance, and experience presents an opportunity for spiritual growth. You'll realize that you have within you the power to do whatever is necessary to change the areas of your life that no longer serve you. When you decide to embrace this truth there's a good chance that you'll feel some trepidation. More than likely, you'll be faced with the reality that you've made some less than desirable choices, perhaps by staying in a relationship that undermines your self-esteem, or overspending and accumulating too much debt. These choices may challenge you to make changes that feel overwhelming or a little scary. For example, you may need to seriously reconsider an important relationship or stay in an unsatisfying job while you whittle away at the debt you've accumulated over the years.

As challenging as it might be, it's important for you to take ownership of your present circumstances. When you're immersed in the pain of your discontent, all options seem to disappear. For example, if you work full time, care for an elderly parent, and struggle to pay your bills, you may feel hopeless about changing your situation. When you can't see your options clearly and you're totally frustrated, it's only natural to feel like a victim of circumstance. When you claim ownership of your life, however, you stop giving your creative energy to outside sources and start using your internal resources to move you in the right direction. You begin to see every circumstance as an opportunity to evolve and grow. When you view life from this perspective you always have options. For example, you might decide to use the situation with your elderly parent as an opportunity to practice asking for and receiving help. From the perspective of an artist, you'll soon find that anything is possible!

Here's some good news that should motivate you: When you take ownership of your life, you engage a powerful Divine force to support your efforts. This force will bring you exactly what you need to make the changes that will improve your life. And you don't have to believe it for it to work. Time and again I've seen the strongest disbeliever be given the gift of an open door at exactly the moment he or she needed one. I remember the surprise of one skeptical client in particular who received an unexpected phone call from a previous employer asking him to rejoin the firm *the day after* he had been laid off from his job. To this day he still talks about it with amazement!

You'll have a great opportunity to practice using your creativity if you've heard yourself say:

- Things always turn out wrong for me.
- Yes, but . . .
- I need someone to bail me out.
- Life is not fair, this always happens to me.
- You don't understand. This has nothing to do with me, it's ____'s fault.
- I don't want to be a grown-up.
- Why bother . . .
- I'm just not a lucky person.
- I can't help it; my situation is unique.

If you recognize yourself in the above phrases, don't worry. Self-awareness is the first step on the road to reclaiming ownership of your life. You simply need a reminder of how powerful you really are. Let me tell you about two simple exercises that demonstrate my point.

One early June weekend I had the privilege of speaking at Mile Hi church in Lakewood, Colorado. When my event was completed, I spent some time with Karen Thomas, the activities and events director. During our conversation Karen mentioned that Richard Bach, the author of the bestseller *Jonathan Liv-*

ingston Seagull (among many others), had recently visited the church to conduct a weekend workshop. When I mentioned that I was a fan of his work, she handed me the audiotapes recorded during his program. It was such a pleasure to listen to him again.

While riding in my car I paid attention as Richard spoke about a little exercise that he used to remind himself of his ability to create his own reality. Richard said he would choose an object, any random object, and firmly hold an image of this object in mind. Then, once he was able to see this object clearly, he let it go, affirming that it was now moving toward him. He then waited for the image to appear in some form in his life.

Although this exercise seemed simplistic to me, I decided to give it a try and was quite surprised by the results. I pulled over, closed my eyes, and envisioned a plump, ripe, red tomato. Once I saw the tomato in my mind's eye, I let it go and got back onto the highway to get to my meeting. As I listened to the radio, I occasionally thought about this image. One hour into my drive, a truck in front of me moved into the right lane and, as I passed it, I noticed a larger-than-life, plump, ripe, red tomato painted on its side. Hmm, I thought, this stuff just might work.

Being a skeptic, I decided to give it another try. This time I envisioned a Rolls-Royce (a car that is not seen frequently in the part of the country in which I live). With the image firmly in mind, I quickly let it go. The next morning, while driving home from visiting a friend, I not only saw one Rolls-Royce, but two within 30 minutes of each other!

What do a tomato and a Rolls-Royce have to do with your power to create your life? *Your thoughts are like magnets.* What you think about and focus your attention on shows up in your life. When you focus your emotional and mental energy on a particular thought, you draw the physical manifestation of that thought toward you. For example, have you ever noticed how, when you learn a new word, you begin to see that word everywhere? Or when you start wearing a new color it suddenly seems as though everyone is wearing it? These are small reminders of a greater spiritual principle—*your thoughts shape your life!*

Why not give this little exercise a try? Even though it may seem silly or even a little strange, stop right now and choose an image, any image, regardless of how unusual it might be. Once you have one, spend a few moments seeing it clearly in your mind. Give power to this image by "expecting" to see it with gentle confidence. Then, let it go. Throughout the day allow this image to creep into your mind, but don't work too hard to see it again. Just relax and notice it. Keep track of how long it takes for this image to appear in your life. It might take an hour, a day, or even a week. Just remain open to seeing it. I've found that the more I practice this exercise, the quicker objects appear. After a few successful attempts, you'll begin to understand what a powerful artist you truly are.

Take Action! Picture This

Now let's apply this same concept to an area of your life that you'd like to change so you can strengthen this new belief even further. For example, if something isn't working in your life, stop, envision a new outcome, and consistently return to this image when your mind fills with fear or resignation. Pick a specific area now:

The area of my life I'd like to change is:

_____

_____

The new outcome I'd like to envision is:

_____

_____

Once you have a new image, focus your mind intently on it, to the point when you actually can *feel* what it would be like to experience this new reality in your life. Then, answer the following questions:

How would your life be different with this new outcome?

_____

_____

How would this new outcome serve you?

_____

_____

If you have a hard time holding this image in your mind (don't worry, many people do), then do this next exercise:

To help you envision your new outcome, write about it in detail here:

_____

_____

_____

_____

Once you've written in detail about the new situation or experience you're ready to boil these details down into one specific, positive sentence. But first, let's look at an example.

When Dalia complained about the hopelessness of finding a baby-sitter for her three small boys, I decided to use these exercises as a way to remind her of who's in charge. As is often the case with baby-sitters, each time she found someone she liked, something would happen to end the arrangement. The first baby-sitter found a job at a local restaurant. The second moved to a new city. Her third attempt ended when the baby-sitter decided to work full time for a neighbor. Needless to say, Dalia felt frustrated and resigned herself to toughing it out on her own. When I invited her to reinstate a sense of hope by writing down her new intention, this is what she said:

> *I want to have enough baby-sitters so I don't have to worry about one leaving and throwing my schedule into an upheaval. I want these women to look forward to being with my children. They need to be responsible and loving, and I want my boys to enjoy their company. I also want them to be dependable, affordable, and enthusiastic about getting started.*

Now that she was clear about her intention, I helped her to boil this intention down into one sentence. Her sentence looked like this:

> *I have a reserve of responsible and dependable baby-sitters who lovingly care for my sons with joy and ease.*

Dalia was then ready for the next step. I had her write this sentence in her journal 15 times. Years ago I adopted this exercise from Scott Adams (the *Dilbert* cartoonist), who said that when he really wanted something to happen in his life, he wrote out the specific request in one sentence at least 15 times. Always open to trying new ideas from successful people, I began to incorporate this exercise into my life. Any time I wanted to create a specific outcome, I would write a sentence that represented this desire in my journal (or on a piece of paper) at least 15 times. Then I added my own finishing touch—I said a little prayer I always use when I set my intentions: "Dear God, please allow this or something better to come into my life." As I write each sentence, I imagine that I am deepening a groove in the record of my mind. And, as this groove gets deeper, I am drawing the end result toward me little by little with each completed sentence.

Now it's your turn. Write your one sentence here:

_____

Now that you have a clear intention of how you'd like this specific situation to change, copy this sentence into your journal at least 15 times.

Once Dalia was clear about what she wanted to create in her life, her work didn't stop there. These exercises are not intended to be magic. They are intended to orient your mind in the direction of your desires. *A strong mind is the first defense against feeling like a victim.* Dalia set about spreading the word in her neighborhood, telling all of her friends that she was intent on finding at least three new baby-sitters for her boys. She hung up a flyer at her children's school, her local library, and on her church bulletin board. One week later she was contacted by a local college student who needed extra money and was available to watch her boys two afternoons each week. Once the girl started, she mentioned a friend who also needed money. This friend was studying child development and loved children. Dalia quickly had baby-sitter number two. At this point, Dalia began to take ownership of the power she had to tackle any situation, regardless of how insurmountable or frustrating it might seem.

Although these exercises may seem simplistic, I've seen them work time and again, both in my own life and in the lives of my clients. More often than not I've been amazed at the end result. I invite you to put your skepticism aside and give it a try. Think of it as an experiment. When your analytical mind steps in and tells you that this exercise is crazy, just smile and let the thought go. If you practice these two simple exercises, you just might become a believer too!

It might be hard to believe that your thoughts, emotions, and energy dictate your life experience, but I'm sure you've seen it play out before. For example, how often have you started the day off on the wrong foot, only to have one challenging experience after another? You wake up late, and as you rush to get ready for work, your negative thinking draws every possible frustration toward you. Getting dressed you pop a button on your shirt, and proceed to beat yourself up for not getting to bed earlier. Your frustration creates more frazzle and you start to misplace things, like your car keys or important papers for work. When you finally leave home you realize on the way that you've left your daily planner behind. Your negative thinking, which started when you woke up, fuels your emotions and influences your energy, drawing toward you the very thing you don't want—more frustration.

By owning the creative power of your thoughts you recognize that your negative thinking brought you to this point. With this realization, you (1) stop for a moment and breathe; (2) assess the situation; and (3) shift your perspective, knowing that you can create a different outcome by thinking different thoughts.

I've seen the same situation happen in positive ways too. I remember one day in particular. I woke up in a great mood and headed for the shower. Once inside I noticed that I had run out of my favorite lavender soap—a scent that I love—so I made a mental note to get more. When I left the house I noticed my neighbor's garden and made another mental note to pick up fresh flowers.

I went about my morning, and on my way home stopped at the post office to pick up my mail. Along with several letters was a small box. I arrived home just in time to find a florist's truck in my driveway. A friend unexpectedly had sent me a beautiful bouquet of orchids (one of my favorites). I was quite surprised by the synchronicity of this event. I suddenly had a sense of being "in the flow." As I sat down to open my mail, I started with the small box. When I opened the package I was shocked to find several bars of sweet-smelling lavender soap. In that moment I smiled to myself, knowing that while these events might seem unrelated to others, I'd come to recognize them as an indication of how powerful my thoughts and intentions really are. Being in the right state of mind created the right atmosphere and energy to draw toward me what I needed.

PAY ATTENTION!

As you begin to see your life from the viewpoint of an artist, recognizing that your outer world is simply a reflection of your inner world, a world that you dictate, you're ready to adopt what I call a "self-reflective reflex." This reflex means that you begin to view your world from the perspective of "everything that occurs is a result of my intention and therefore an opportunity for me to develop my spiritual character."

With this perspective in mind, you naturally begin to view each life experience through the lens of the question "How can I use this situation to serve my personal growth?" For example, when a driver cuts you off in traffic, you see it as a sign that you may need to slow down or not take things so personally, rather than view it as someone doing something to you. Or when you lose your job unexpectedly, you decide to reevaluate the direction of your life's work instead of seeing it as life handing you a raw deal. Of course it's important to allow yourself to experience and express all of the feelings that accompany these types of situations. The point is to move beyond blame and criticism to a more empowering position—one where you recognize that you have the creative power to use any situation to your advantage.

For years I've practiced this self-reflective reflex. I've trained myself to take ownership of my creative power by viewing every life experience as an opportunity to grow and learn. When something happens that causes any kind of reaction, I automatically ask myself the following questions:

Why have I drawn this experience to me at this time?

What is this experience trying to teach me?

How can I use this situation to make me a better person?

My friend Fran learned a lot from asking these questions when she was faced with helping a dying friend to settle her affairs. Fran was afraid of death and knew that this was one of the reasons why she had called this experience into her life. Participating in the end of her friend's life was an extraordinary journey that taught Fran a lot about herself. She no longer saw death as something to fear but something to celebrate. And she came away from the experience stronger, more committed to living a life that honored her most treasured priorities.

Awareness in and of itself can be a powerful force for change. By asking yourself the above questions, you automatically put yourself in a position of power—someone who has control over his or her life.

Taking ownership of your life and recognizing that your thoughts and intentions directly influence your life experiences is the first step in making a conscious commitment to your spiritual evolution. As you work through the program outlined in this book, you'll have an opportunity to continue this work in a deeper way.

TURN YOUR VISION INWARD

The key to building the confidence and self-esteem you'll need to lead your life lies in developing a strong relationship with yourself. To do this you must defy society's pull toward preoccupation with what's happening "out there" by turning your vision inward.

We live in a world that constantly pulls us outside of ourselves. There are the sensational news stories, larger than life film characters, nonstop advertisements on television, radio, the Internet, and in the mail. And there are the individual distractions as well—earning a living, raising the kids, company politics, keeping up with the Joneses—you get the picture. We also tend to focus our attention on everything but the present moment. We're either pulled back into the past or forward into the future, never living in the "now." The problem with this perspective is that within the present moment lies the opportunity to use our most potent creative power. The more we live outside of the present moment, the more attached we become to external results, accomplishments, possessions, or the opinions of others.

A commitment to turning your vision inward on a regular basis will train you to look inside for answers. When you do, you'll begin to make the highest spiritual choices for your life. By engaging in activities that draw you closer to yourself, you not only create a strong attachment to your inner world, you learn that *you can trust yourself to handle any situation.* A solid, positive relationship with yourself is essential. There are no shortcuts, no quick fixes, and no easy antidotes. The journey to self-confidence and courage begins and ends with you.

It's so ironic that the very thing we need to do to build a strong foundation of confidence and self-esteem is so simple—we need to spend time with ourselves. Each one of us has our own unique way of developing a stronger connection to our spiritual center. The method may be different, but the goal is the same: You need to spend consistent time in communion with yourself. The way you do this is less important than the commitment you make to a regular practice. I'm always surprised at how people know exactly what they need to do to develop a stronger relationship with themselves; it's doing it that's the problem. For example, I always trust the wisdom of my clients. When I want to know a client's unique path inward, I simply ask the following question:

What's the one activity you know you need to do every day that would strengthen your relationship with yourself?

When I ask this question, I hear a variety of responses. See if anything appeals to you:

Walk

Journal

Exercise

Cook

Do nothing

Listen to music

Meditate/spend time reflecting

Do something creative: draw, paint, sing, dance, etc.

Take a bath

Spend time alone in a favorite place in nature

How do you connect with yourself and your spiritual center? For years I've kept a journal. I know without a doubt that this single activity returns me to center quicker than anything else does. When I journal I engage in a dialogue with myself. I capture my feelings, reactions, needs, wants, desires, fears, etc., on the page. When I practice this activity consistently I feel more confident, more connected to my priorities, I make better choices, and I feel a sense of inner security that nothing outside of me has ever replaced.

What activity does this for you? The goal in committing to a daily practice is to build an alliance with yourself. As clichéd as it may sound, you want to become your own best friend— someone you can rely on and turn to in any situation. This one simple action can have a profound effect on your sense of self-worth and self-esteem. But it takes commitment and self-discipline to make it happen.

To begin this process, answer the question for yourself:

What's the one activity you know you need to do every day that would strengthen your relationship with yourself?

Choose one activity that you will engage in every day and write it down here:

_____

As I mentioned earlier, deciding on the activity is far easier than making the commitment to do it every day. So the next step is to determine how you will keep this promise to yourself. What do you need to do to develop the self-discipline to make it happen? How will you bolster your chances of success?

First of all, you need to accept the fact that you will fail to keep this commitment to yourself at one point or another.

When this happens you'll need to have compassion for yourself and simply get right back on track. As you make it a habit to start again, you'll find that the time between stopping and starting gets shorter. Think of self-discipline as an act of self-love. When you engage in any behavior that honors yourself, you automatically raise your self-esteem—the ability to hold yourself in high regard. The way to build this muscle is to keep at it.

The next way to increase your chances of success is to use your partner or support team to help keep you on track. Make a verbal commitment and arrange to use check-in calls for the first 30 days, so you can use this accountability to stay focused.

Finally, create a regular schedule. The body quickly adapts to (and prefers) a routine. When you schedule your daily activity at the same time each day, you'll find yourself naturally gravitating toward that commitment. Think of this routine as a groove that you're creating for yourself. The deeper the groove, the easier it is to stay on track. Mark the time on your calendar and hold it as sacred. Don't let other events or people intrude on this commitment.

Now that you have a daily activity in place, you're ready for the next step: building a deep sense of inner security.

STILLNESS: THE KEY TO INNER SECURITY

Meditation, the art of tuning in, is the perfect metaphor for shutting out your external world. When we close our eyes we flip a switch that connects us to what's going on inside. Almost instantly we become aware of what we're thinking and how we feel.

Try it right now. Close your eyes and take three slow, deep breaths. Notice this shift in energy in your body and your mind.

See what I mean? When you close your eyes, you shut out the world. From this perspective you begin to notice how you feel and what you think in a way that most of us never acknowledge because of our busy lives. For example, you might notice bodily sensations like the shallowness of your breath or the beating of your heart. You notice sounds that you were oblivious to before, like the hum of your computer or the noise of passing traffic. You notice your thoughts and the busyness of your mind as it worries, plans, or overanalyzes. When you learn to connect with your breath on a regular basis by closing your eyes and breathing deeply, you calm your nervous system. Then, as your mind settles, you learn to enter into a state of thoughtlessness so you can become an objective witness to the present moment.

Meditation can be challenging for those of us who are used to being busy. As technology advances at lightning speed there are more ways than ever for people to make demands on our time and energy. We have voicemail, e-mail, cell phones, beepers, faxes, snail mail, and a myriad of time-management devices. We are bombarded with information and stimuli on a daily basis. For example, *American Demographics* reports that the typical U.S. office worker receives more than 189 messages a day. This type of overstimulation makes it very difficult to settle ourselves long enough to sit with silence.

If you're like most people, I'm sure you've noticed the busyness of your mind when you've tried to get quiet or meditate. As soon as you close your eyes and breathe your mind quickly pulls you back outside by reminding you of what needs to be done (future focus) or of what didn't get done (past focus). It's this kind of frenetic overanalyzing that keeps people from using this important tool.

You don't have to go on a month-long silent retreat or move to India to learn how to be still. There are simple ways to begin experiencing the power of stillness right now. For example, when waiting in line at the grocery store, gently close your eyes for several seconds and repeat to yourself: "May I feel calm. May I feel peace. May I feel relaxed." You can use this same exercise when stuck in traffic or faced with a challenging problem at work.

The Institute of Heartmath is a non-profit organization that offers a variety of tools to calm the mind and reduce stress. For example, they have a very useful technique called Freeze-Frame that can help you to settle your mind by shifting your focus to your heart. To do this, draw your attention away from your mind by gently placing your hand over your heart. As you breathe, imagine your breath coming in and out through your heart instead of through your nose or mouth. Then, recall a positive, pleasurable memory. Continue to breathe this way for as long as time allows. By doing this exercise you'll not only calm your mind, you'll regulate your heart rhythms and improve brain function too!

One of my favorite exercises for turning inward is found in *The Power of Now*, by Eckhart Tolle. Tolle offers a great little experiment for experiencing the present moment. He says: "Close your eyes and say to yourself: 'I wonder what my next thought is going to be.' Then become very alert and wait for the next thought. Be like a cat watching a mouse hole. What thought is going to come out of the mouse hole?"

If, when you try this experiment, you find it difficult to stay in the present moment, gently continue to repeat the phrase "I wonder what my next thought is going to be." Sit and wait patiently for even a fleeting moment of present awareness. With practice, you'll find it much easier to reside in this place.

When I first tried this experiment I immediately understood what Tolle was writing about. When you become a highly alert observer of your thoughts you can't help but enter into a state of present-focused awareness. This state is timeless and pain-free. By practicing this simple exercise you can strengthen your mind's ability to reside in this grace-filled place, the place that will always return you to your power.

It's amazing how little time we spend in the quietness of our inner selves. Often, when I ask audiences to close their eyes for five minutes during a workshop to connect with the voice of their soul, a large percentage of the people in the room begin to cry. I find this a potent indication of how little we listen to ourselves.

Experience has taught me that most people need some kind of guidance when first practicing the skill of meditation. I often recommend short (ten-to-fifteen-minute) guided relaxation tapes to help facilitate this process. If you're someone who has a busy mind (who doesn't?), then this may be the best way for you to train yourself to focus and settle down. Too often we get bombarded with self-defeating thoughts when we first try to meditate. The goal is to make the practice of meditation a welcomed event, not a chore to be avoided. Guided relaxation tapes help lead your mind into a relaxed state by using the comfort of a soothing voice. As you teach your mind to listen, it quickly learns to follow your lead. You'll find resources for tapes and CDs at the end of this chapter.

Take Action! Learn to Be Still

To help you get comfortable with the practice of going inside, I'd like to offer you a simple exercise. The following meditation is designed to build your "inner focus muscles." Rather than offer you a script to follow, I'd like to give you something you can use anytime, anywhere—a process of recall. To do this, sit comfortably in a chair, or lie on the floor with your knees bent. Focus on your breath in a way that feels comfortable to you. Don't worry about breathing the *right* way. Trust yourself to know what you need in order to feel relaxed. When you're ready, follow this three-step process:

1. Take several breaths and let yourself relax.

2. Spend five minutes recalling a favorite memory in detail. For example, you might replay your wedding day in your mind's eye, see yourself playing softball with a group of friends during a summer picnic, or watch your son or daughter take his or her first step. As you recall these events, allow yourself to see, hear, feel, and smell the whole scene in vivid detail. When you're finished, go on to step three.

3. Take a few deep breaths and return to your body.

The idea behind this exercise is to teach you to control your thoughts while sitting still. You can vary the second step in a number of ways. For example, you might imagine yourself doing something you love to do, like painting, swimming, or running through your favorite park. As you do this exercise be sure to allow your mind to relive this experience in full detail. How did you feel? What did you see? What did you hear? Bask in the joy of remembering this event. Using a specific focus in the early stages of your meditation practice makes sitting still easier. As you practice this skill, you'll find it much easier to shift to sitting in silence, letting your thoughts gently drift away, so you can experience the present moment.

Meditation has many benefits. For example, it teaches you to take control of your thinking so you can focus your mind. It improves your ability to visualize—an important skill for an artist to develop. Meditation also has numerous physical benefits. It helps you to relax and reduce stress. It decreases cortisol levels (a hormone that is released during times of stress), strengthens immune function, and has been successfully used in the treatment of chronic pain.

Most important of all, learning to meditate will give you an experience of connecting with a presence larger and more powerful than your individual self. When this happens you'll suddenly understand the value of this important practice. As you connect with a universal, collective consciousness, you tap into a wealth of power and peace that builds a sense of inner security. As you return to this place of power, you build self-trust.

LEARN TO TRUST YOURSELF

Learning to trust yourself is an integral part of building a strong foundation that will allow you to lead your life. When I looked up the definition of trust in the dictionary, I found a perfect prescription: "Trust is a reliance on the integrity, veracity, or reliability of a person. Trust is something committed to one's care for use or safekeeping." In other words, you learn to trust yourself when you behave in ways that honor and care for who you are.

How trustworthy are you? To find out, score yourself by answering the following questions:

- How well do you honor your needs? Do you sleep when you're tired, eat when you're hungry, or take a break when you're feeling stressed? Rate yourself on a scale from one to ten with one representing "not at all" and ten representing "all the time".

    1–2–3–4–5–6–7–8–9–10

- When you make promises to yourself do you keep them? For example, if you promise yourself that you'll spend a quiet evening alone reading a favorite book, do you cancel it when an unexpected invitation comes along?

    1–2–3–4–5–6–7–8–9–10

- Can you trust yourself to make tough choices? For example, will you walk away from a relationship that weakens your self-esteem or leave a job that pays the bills but leaves you feeling unfulfilled?

    1–2–3–4–5–6–7–8–9–10

- Do you stand up for yourself when someone steps over your boundaries or acts in an inappropriate way? For example, can you tell a friend that it's not okay to tease, judge, or criticize you?

    1–2–3–4–5–6–7–8–9–10

What have you learned about yourself and your level of trustworthiness? Write about the changes you need to make in order to become more trustworthy in your journal.

The ability to stand in your own spotlight comes from developing a solid foundation of inner security—a belief in yourself and the vision you have for your life. You must act in ways that make it clear to your own needs and desires that you are trustworthy. When you develop this kind of trust, you are better able to tune in to how you really feel and use these feelings to guide your choices—choices that evoke self-respect. As this happens you become less attached to the opinions of others and more able to make the decisions that support what you want and need. One of the ways in which we identify our needs is by tuning in to how we feel.

DO LESS, FEEL MORE

Many of us struggle to keep up with society's pace. High-speed computers and quicker Internet access force our minds and bodies to adjust to increasing speeds. The sound bite and sidebar strategies of advertising companies and the news media overstimulate our nervous systems on a daily basis. For example, while watching CNN or other news programs, you can now check stock prices, sports scores, and other late-breaking news all at the same time.

As we consider the reality of how hard it is to stay connected to our inner lives, we're all faced with a fundamental truth: *We live in a world that forces us to shut down the very thing we need in order to experience deep meaning and fulfillment—an ability to stay connected to how we feel.*

Most of us are constantly living in our heads—thinking, calculating, anticipating, multitasking, analyzing, and doing, doing,

doing. This overfocus on information has placed a high value on what we *know* instead of how we *feel*. Unfortunately, the experience of leading a rich and fulfilling life comes not through thinking, but through feeling. For example, when you get together with your friends, it's probably not your conversation about politics or work that gives you a sense of connection, it's the feeling of joy and camaraderie you get from being in their presence. Your conversation may be intellectually stimulating, but isn't it the laughter, the love, and the feeling of being connected that you most often remember?

Feelings are your inner guidance system—your emotional compass. When you allow this compass to direct your actions you build self-trust. When you feel hungry, you eat. When you feel tired, you rest. When you feel lonely, you reach out for connection to others. In this most basic way your feelings link you with the wisest part of yourself. They tell you what you need to know at any given moment.

I am always so touched by the people who come up to me after a presentation to share their personal stories. Often, as someone starts to cry while relaying the details of a particular situation, they go out of their way to apologize for their tears. I usually stop them and offer a gentle reminder that crying is good. I've come to see tears as a sign that our soul is trying to tell us something important. When given permission to relax into their feelings, I actually can see the relief wash over their body.

Many of us learn to shut off our feelings early in life. Girls are typically taught to stop crying or refrain from being so sensitive, while boys are taught to "suck it up." This callous disregard for our emotions has left most of us sleepwalking through life.

When we are disconnected from our emotional center—our inner compass—it's only natural that we feel lost.

Opening your heart and allowing yourself to feel can be frightening at first. As you do this there's a good chance that you may experience moments of sadness, guilt, fear, anger, or other uncomfortable emotions. That's why so many people flee from connecting with how they feel. In my own life I've learned that suffering comes more from repressing how I feel than from the act of feeling in and of itself. In fact, when we neglect to express our feelings fully, those buried emotions can take a heavy toll on our health. Swallowing anger, sadness, or bitterness and carrying this heavy baggage in our bodies can result in everything from depression and physical illness to even death.

Our unexpressed emotions can also become toxic obstacles that prevent us from moving forward with our lives. I remember an example of this from a woman who was courageous enough to stand up during a seminar and admit that her anger had become so overpowering that she was unable to connect with any positive feelings. She said: "I realize my unexpressed anger is what's preventing me from connecting with my passion. I've got all this rage inside and I just don't know how to get past it."

CONNECTING WITH HOW YOU FEEL

How do we begin to connect with our emotions? I recommend that you develop three specific habits. First, you need to stop "doing" so much. You need to build in regular downtime during the day so you can rest and be present with yourself. Second, you have to create a reflex of checking in with yourself in a conscious way. And finally, you need to find a "safe mirror," someone you trust who will encourage you to express how you feel from a deeper, more soulful place while they listen with openness and love.

Take Action! Keep a Mood Journal to Connect with How You Feel

For the next week, keep a mood journal. Take your journal (or a small notebook) with you and, as you go about your day, stop at random times to rest and check in with how you feel. Make sure you record what you *feel,* not what you *think.* You might take some time upon wakening, at lunch, or in midafternoon when you could use a break. To do this, copy the following questions into your journal and use them each day when you check in with how you feel. Then, as you check in, close your eyes, take a few deep breaths, and ask yourself the following questions:

What am I feeling right now?

What sensations do I notice in my body?

What images come into view?

What are these images or feelings trying to tell me about myself?

Is there something I feel I need or want? If so, what is it?

Isabelle was a client who used the alarm on her wristwatch to teach herself to check in with her feelings. Each hour, when the alarm beeped, she would stop, close her eyes to eliminate any visual distractions, and take note of how she was feeling in that exact moment. She'd then jot down a few sentences about her perceptions. Like any new skill, with consistent practice Isabelle began to notice a stronger connection to her feelings throughout the day whether her alarm went off or not. As a result of this daily practice she recognized a distinct shift in her interactions with others. Isabelle said she felt more connected to loved ones and coworkers and that she began to experience frequent moments of "grace"—feelings of deep gratitude for her life.

Take Action! Schedule Time with a Friend

Spending quality time with a trusted friend or family member is another key way to tune into how you feel. There's nothing better than enjoying a relaxed afternoon or evening of deep conversation with someone who encourages you to reveal your true self. While there are some friends or family members who naturally evoke this type of exchange when you happen to be in their company, it's important to schedule these get-togethers on a regular basis. When you get in the habit of sharing your vulnerability and sensitivity with those you trust, believe me, you become hungry for this type of interaction. Superficial chit-chat gets old real fast. Remember to honor your self by sharing only what feels safe. This is an important way to build self-trust.

I've been blessed with the opportunity to have this type of meaningful contact on a regular basis. Ten years ago I was invited to join a "dialogue group"—a gathering of people who meet with the express intention of communicating from a soulful place. During our dialogue meetings each member is encouraged to share their deepest feelings. There is no seeking of agreement, debating, diagnosing, or fixing allowed. The intention is pure: share who you are in a safe place with friends who will simply witness your authenticity. I am always surprised by the depth of feeling I experience while in the company of these amazing friends. As a result, these gatherings continue to provide some of the most meaningful and richest experiences of my life.

Who will you share your feelings with? How often will you meet? Maybe it's your partner or someone from your Life Makeover Group. You might even decide to use one of your meetings to conduct your own dialogue group. For example, gather together and open your meeting with five or ten minutes of meditation. Then, when moved to do so, speak from a deep place and express how you feel in the moment. Give each person a chance to talk while other members simply witness the remarks. When done, conclude the meeting with a few minutes of silence to honor your time together.

Take Action! Heal Your Emotional Blocks

As you become more connected to how you feel, there's a good chance that you might stumble upon emotional issues that need to be addressed. There may be unresolved anger or grief with a family member, or a painful memory that suddenly comes to the surface. When this happens it's important to stay connected to how you feel. Don't go back under, or attempt to ignore these feelings. As one very wise woman said on one of our Lifestyle Makeover shows: "Your pain always waits for you."

I would not be where I am today had I not had the support and guidance of a *good* therapist. I use the word "good" intentionally. Too many people I've worked with have had unsatisfactory experiences with therapists and end up never getting the help they deserve. When looking for a therapist, start by asking friends, family members, or those people who already provide you with some kind of health care service (doctor, physical therapist, or nurse practitioner) for referrals.

When you find a therapist be sure to interview them before making a decision. Ask about their educational background and experience. For example, if you decide to deal with issues related to your marriage or family, be sure that the therapist has specific training in this area. Also, ask about their preferred method of treatment. Describe your current circumstances to see how the therapist might recommend you use his or her services to your best advantage.

Ask for what you want. Experience has taught me that most clients prefer a therapist who has a more directive, action-oriented approach. Don't be afraid to get all the details you need before making a decision. And be willing to interview as many therapists as it takes to find the right one. Don't be afraid to ask for a trial period to see if it's a good match. You should feel a sense of comfort and excitement at the thought of working with this person. Remember: Do not give your power away to someone just because they have a degree in counseling. Therapists are people just like you.

Take Action! Scan Your Day for Emotions

Another way to reconnect with your feelings is by reviewing your day with your eye on connecting feelings to specific events. When you write about an event from this perspective, you suddenly drop below the surface of objectively reporting it, and you begin to connect with the experience on a deeper level. Start today by answering the following questions in your journal:

- What significant event(s) occurred today? (I had a great conversation with my best friend, visited with my grandmother who drives me crazy, or spoke up too forcefully in a team meeting)
- How did these events make me feel? What were my reactions?

You can also keep track of your dreams. Dreams can become a window that provides a wonderful view into your interior life. When you wake up in the morning, simply scribble notes about what you remember as well as any feelings that the dream may have left you with. Over time, as you continue to pay attention to the images and feelings that your dreamlife has to offer, you'll not only remember more of your dreams, you'll begin to connect your feelings with messages from your subconscious.

Here are a few other ways to connect with how you feel:

- Therapeutic massage.
- Body-centered psychotherapy (therapy that includes body-work to release blocked emotions in the body).

- Psycho-drama (an action-based form of therapy in which people dramatize their issues and resolutions).

- Improvisational acting classes.

- Spending time with children.

Now that you've begun this important journey into developing a deeper, more meaningful relationship with yourself, remember these five important messages:

- Your thoughts are like magnets. They will shape your life.

- Spend regular time with yourself.

- Slow down. Do less and feel more.

- Create and keep daily habits to build a solid foundation of self-trust.

- You always have options.

As you review these five messages, what three actions are you willing to take:

1. _____

2. _____

3. _____

As you continue to take action on this journey, you'll be better able to answer the question "Who do you think you are?"

RESOURCES

Books

The Power of Now: A Guide to Spiritual Enlightenment by Eckhart Tolle (New World Library, 1999)
Eckhart Tolle's message is simple: living in the *now* is the truest path to happiness and enlightenment.

The Secret of the Shadow: The Power of Owning Your Whole Story by Debbie Ford (Harper San Francisco, 2001)
Debbie Ford shows you how to rediscover your true essence hidden in the shadow of your dramatic life story.

The Heart of the Soul: Emotional Awareness by Gary Zukav and Linda Francis (Simon & Schuster, 2002)
Gary Zukav and Linda Francis will teach you how to cultivate a relationship with your heart so you can live in alignment with your soul.

Sark's Journal and Play! Book: A Place to Dream While Awake by SARK (Celestial Arts, 1993)
This unique journal is spacious, carefree, fun, colorful, and a wonderful place to make a record of you.

Self Matters: Creating Your Life From Inside Out by Phillip C. McGraw (Simon & Schuster, 2001)
Dr. Phil challenges you to find your "authentic self"—that person you once were before life took its toll.

Divine Intuition: Your Guide to Creating a Life You Love by Lynn A. Robinson (DK Publishing, 2001)
This beautifully illustrated book will help you to develop an inner resource (your intuition) that will give you unfailing direction toward your hopes and dreams.

Life Is Not a Stress Rehearsal by Loretta LaRoche
Loretta's book provides a great way to reduce stress and have a good laugh, while seriously reconsidering your priorities.

Jonathan Livingston Seagull by Richard Bach (Avon, 1995)
A wonderful fable about the importance of seeking a higher purpose.

Guided Relaxation Resources

www.serenitymusic.com
This is a terrific website for relaxation tapes, CDs, and tools that impart a special feeling of inner peace to the listener. Check out *The Healing Waterfall* with narration by actress Jill Andre and music by Max Highstein!

Ten Minutes to Relax by Paul Overman (Relaxation Co., 1999)
These short meditations are a simple way to learn to still your mind and relax.

Morning and Evening Meditations and Prayers by Joan Borysenko (Hay House, 1997)
This audiotape is filled with beautiful meditations that help you to begin and end each day.

Morning and Evening: Music, Meditation and Prayer by Marianne Williamson (Hay House, 1997)
This tape lets you start the day with hope and optimism, and end the day with a feeling of peace, relaxation, and satisfaction.

Other

Go Goddess Games
www.gogoddess.com
(305) 661–6167
Go Goddess! Is a board game that provides an entertaining forum for women to freely express their thoughts and dreams with open, honest communication.

www.comfortqueen.com
206–780–5445
This website offers lovely journals for your daily writing as well as other self-care items.

Tools With Heart
www.toolswithheart.com
888-2-JOURNAL
888-256-8762
Tools With Heart offers a beautiful collection of thematic journals made from handmade paper and book cloth, writing accessories, and relaxation tools.

CHAPTER TWO

Define Your Values

Y EARS AGO WHILE COMPLETING my coach training
at an organization called Coach U, I was introduced to
a program that taught me a lot about myself. One of
the underlying philosophies at Coach U is that in order for
coaches to best serve their clients, they must be actively engaged
in improving the quality of their own lives. In keeping with that
philosophy, coaches were expected to complete the self-
development programs and use the assessment tests that would
eventually be used by clients.

One of these programs was called the "Tru Values Program." It was designed to help people discover their core values
so that they could begin to orient their lives around what really
mattered. Values represent the very essence of what's most important to us in life. When I completed the assessment test I
suddenly saw with great clarity the correlation between what I
valued and my Divine assignment. Looking back, it was the first
real glimpse I had into how I might use my talents and gifts in
service to others.

When I work with clients to help them identify their values, they begin to reconnect with themselves in a deep and

meaningful way. Life starts to make sense. A direction begins to reveal itself. And they begin to feel a sense of realignment that helps them to see where they should (and should not) be spending their precious time and energy.

As you continue to rediscover yourself by exploring your inner landscape, clarifying your values can help you to understand yourself on a much deeper, more spiritual level.

Take Action! Identify Your Essential Values

I'd like to help you identify your values. Following is a random list of words—nouns, verbs, or phrases—for you to read through. As you look over the list, I want you to circle any word or phrase that feels important to you. Pay special attention to those words that seem to jump out and choose you or to the words that just feel right to you. Watch your tendency to choose words that you feel you *should* choose versus the ones that *you* really want to choose. Circle any word that speaks to the essence of who you are. And, don't think too much. You might even close your eyes, take a few deep breaths, establish a connection between your head and your heart, and respond from this place.

The Values List

Abundance	Articulate	Augment	Be connected
Accomplish	Artistic	Awe	Be integrated
Acquire	Assemble	Be accepting	Be joyful
Adventure	Assist	Be amused	Be linked
Alert	Attain	Be awake	Be passionate
Alter	Attentive	Be aware	Be present
Arouse	Attract	Be bonded	Be sensitive

Be spiritual	Detect	Facilitate	Ingenuity
Beauty	Devotion	Family	Inquisitive
Bliss	Direct	Foster	Inspire
Bravery	Discern	Freedom	Instruct
Build	Distinguish	Fun	Integrate
Calm	Drama	Gamble	Integrity
Capable	Dream	Glamor	Invent
Cause	Educate	Govern	Laugh
Coach	Elegance	Grace	Learn
Comfort	Emphasize	Grant	Love
Community	Encourage	Gratitude	Magnificence
Compassionate	Endeavor	Greatest	Mastery
Complete	Endow	Guide	Minister
Conceive	Energize	Have fun	Model
Congruent	Energy	Health	Move forward
Connection	Energy flow	Holy	Observe
Contentment	Enjoy	Honest	Open minded
Control	Enlighten	Honoring	Orchestrate
Courage	Enroll	Humor	Originality
Danger	Entertain	Imagination	Outdo
Dare	Excellence	Impact	Patient
Dedication	Exhilaration	Improve	Peaceful
Delight	Experiment	In touch with	People
Dependable	Expert	Influence	Perceive
Design	Explain	Inform	Perfect

Persevere	Rule	Stimulate	To relate
Persuade	Satisfied	Strengthen	To teach
Plan	Score	Superiority	To unite
Play games	Security	Support	To win
Playful	See	Synthesize	Touch
Pleasure	Seek	Taste	Transform
Prepare	Sensation	Tenderness	Triumph
Prevail	Sense	The unknown	Trustworthy
Provide	Sensual	Thoughtful	Truth
Quest	Serenity	Thrill	Turn
Radiance	Serve	To catalyze	Uncover
Realize	Set standards	To contribute	Understand
Refine	Sex	To create	Unique
Reign	Sincere	To discover	Uplift
Relate to God	Space	To experience	Unstick others
Religious	Spark	To feel	Venture
Respond	Speculate	To feel good	Vulnerable
Responsible	Spirit	To glow	Wealth
Risk	Spontaneous	To lead	Win over
Romance	Sports	To nurture	

Once you've circled all the words and phrases you want, add any additional words or phrases that you feel are important that may not have been on this list:

1. _____

2. _____

3. _____

4. _____

5. _____

Now that you've chosen all the words/phrases that are important to you, I'd like you to narrow this list down to ten. Review each circled word and put a check mark next to the ones that feel *really* important. Once you've done that, choose ten and list them here:

1. _____   6. _____

2. _____   7. _____

3. _____   8. _____

4. _____   9. _____

5. _____   10. _____

Look over this list carefully. How does it make you feel when you read these words? Do they seem to represent a deep part of you? Do they represent someone you aspire to be or something you aspire to do? Do you feel a sense of hope or excitement as you look at this list?

Now it's time to narrow them down even further. As you look over your list of ten, I'd like you to choose the four words that are the most important of all. Some people know them immediately, while others feel frustrated and uncomfortable with the idea of giving up the other six. Relax, there is no perfect answer. Your values may very well shift over time as you come to know yourself on a deeper level. To make the process easier, look for a word that seems to encompass another. For example, if you've chosen the words "inspire" and "influence" you might decide to choose "inspire" because it naturally expresses your value of "influence." Whatever your response, take your time and choose only four—the four words or phrases that best represent the essence of you now. Ready? Narrow them down and list your four essential values here:

1. _____
2. _____
3. _____
4. _____

As you look over this list, how do the words or phrases make you feel? Do they make you smile, feel excited, or content? These are your essential values.

As you look over your four values, take some time to answer the following questions in your journal:

- What have you learned about yourself from this exercise?
- How are these values expressed in your life already?
- Which values still need to be expressed in some way?
- When you look back over your life, how have these values influenced your actions?
- How would you describe someone who had these values?

This last question can be used with your partner or Life Makeover Group to gain a new perspective of yourself. For example, you might have each group member print their values on a small piece of paper and bring them to the next meeting. Then put these slips of paper in a basket and have each member choose one. Go around the room and have each person describe the kind of person who would best represent the types of values listed on their sheet. For example, if one member chose the values love, fun, learn and community, you might say something like: "This person is fun-loving and enjoys the company of others. They are open-minded and excited to learn new things. They probably place a high value on family and may even be heavily involved in their community."

Some clients say that once they've clarified their values they feel a deep sense of knowing in their body. I've heard things like: "Yes, that's definitely me!" or "I feel like I've come home."

Some clients say they feel "realigned" or "oriented in a new way." One woman told me, "I now have a clear sense of direction." Other clients experience a deep sadness when they realize that the lives they're living have nothing to do with the values they've uncovered.

The words you've chosen as your values may in fact represent a need or desire more than an existing value that is expressed in your life. Don't worry. Experience has taught me that initially, whether your values represent a need, desire, or true expression of a particular gift, they always symbolize something that relates to your Divine assignment—your personal and spiritual development and your way of being of service to others.

When I originally did this "values" test myself many years ago, my four essential values were: to inspire, to create, to be connected, and to learn. When I look back I can see clearly how these values were indicative of my future as a writer, community builder, and teacher. At the time, the value of "be connected" was more of a need than a value. I can now see that I chose that word because I needed more community in my life. But from that need grew the desire to create community for others as well. This is now expressed through the development of the Life Makeover Groups and my on-line community.

Your values do not necessarily represent your intended work in the world. They signify those things that you must have in your life in order to be your best. For example, one of my clients who chose the value "beauty," expresses this value by creating beauty in all areas of her life. She always has fresh flowers in her home. She visits beautiful places in nature on a regular basis, and she loves to wear beautiful clothes.

It's always interesting to watch the reactions of people when they narrow their list down to four. I remember the look on a young woman's face when I offered this exercise during a small workshop I was leading in New York. As she went through the process of refining her values, she began to fidget in her seat. When it came time to talk about what she had discovered, she jumped up, listed her four values (excitement, experience, to have fun, and contribution), and said: Now I know why I've enjoyed teaching drama to the young children at my local YWCA. It all makes so much sense. I'm here to share my excitement and enthusiasm for life with others by helping them to have fun! I can also see where I'm wasting my time. I need to stop working at my uncle's law office where I've tried to 'fit in' to a position that does not represent who I really am."

I remember one woman scowling. She said she felt frustrated and confused by her list. As she looked over her values she said that they didn't make any sense. When we went back to explore them together, we discovered that she had chosen words that represented what she thought she should be doing instead of what spoke to her heart and soul.

My client Keith, who had chosen the words "build, drama, to create, and artistic," said that he could see how two of the four words were reflective of his current life (a carpenter and film buff, the words "build and drama" made perfect sense). He recognized that the other two, "to create and artistic," represented values that he longed to express more in his life. Keith made fine objects out of wood and secretly desired to sell them to the general public. He was a terrific artist but had a hard time believing that he was worthy of the title. He said that the exercise had given him the nudge he needed to move forward with bringing his talent out into the world.

While you may feel a resounding "yes!" when you identify your values, there may also be a bit of shyness. When I asked another workshop participant, Maureen, to share her four values with the group, she did so with great reluctance. Her first response was: "These seem like pretty lofty words." As she read them out loud you could see her shrink with each word she uttered. Her values were "inspire, relate to God, to lead, and be passionate." When I asked about her reluctance, she confessed that she felt embarrassed about admitting to values that seemed so big and bold. I understood her reaction. Many of us, when we finally connect with the core of who we are, must face the reality that our spiritual essence is magnificent. Whether your values are more inner oriented like "comfort" or "family," or more outer focused like "to lead" or "to risk," they are equally important. Remember that we've been trained to minimize our greatness so it makes sense that you might feel a bit shy or embarrassed about your values.

What have you discovered about yourself from doing this exercise? Are your values being expressed in your life? If not, how would your life be different if they were? As you continue to go through the program outlined in this book you will gain even more clarity about your true values. For now, I'd like you to put these four words on an index card and keep them in view (on your mirror, the top of your desk, in your wallet, etc.). Sit with them for a while so that the truth can sink in. Feel free to go back and refine them in any way. You'll want to feel a solid *yes* as we move forward.

TIME FOR A CHANGE

Once you're clear about your values, there's a good chance that you'll start to notice how your life needs to change. When this happens you might come up against some resistance. For example, you might hear yourself say something like "everything's just fine the way it is" or "I could never do that because . . ." and "I'm not entitled to have that. . . ." I want to point out that change is something we've been taught to avoid. You've probably heard phrases like "don't ever change," and when you did, you also probably heard the gritting of teeth behind the words sending a message to you that change is bad.

Change is scary because you know what you're giving up, but you don't know, in a visceral sense, what you'll be getting in return. Fear of the unknown is rampant because we all have fabulous imaginations prompted by negativity. Is it possible for you to imagine a positive outcome of change? Even small change?

Take Action! Warm Up to Change

To help prepare you for making the changes that will center your life around your values, let's try a little warm-up exercise. Over the next week, decide to make one simple change every day. For example, you might:

Reverse the order of what you do in the morning.

Eat lunch at a new place.

Try a new food.

Drive home a different way.

Ask for paper instead of plastic at the grocery store (or vice versa).

Wear a different combination of clothes from your closet.

Now it's your turn. What will you do?

Day 1 _____

Day 2 _____

Day 3 _____

Day 4 _____

Day 5 _____

Day 6 _____

Day 7 _____

The idea is to get comfortable with change. Remember that change is usually not as painful as you project it to be. Instead of seeing it as losing something you want or need, decide to see change as getting something great. For example, there is current research that suggests that changing your routine will improve brain function and may even slow down the aging process! When the resistance or fear comes up, lean on your partner or group members for support.

Now that you're on the road to becoming more comfortable with change, let's take the next step. Let's look at some of the changes you may need to make in order to center your life around your values.

DOES YOUR LIFE REFLECT YOUR VALUES?

When you look over your four essential values do you feel satisfied in knowing that they are fully expressed in your life? How might your life need to change? When I did this exercise with Greta, a woman who attended one of my workshops, her ten values looked like this:

1. Love
2. Be joyful
3. Courage
4. Delight
5. Have fun
6. Laugh
7. Learn
8. Peaceful
9. Stimulate
10. Gratitude

When she narrowed it down, her four essential values were:

1. Be joyful
2. Love
3. Learn
4. Courage

Once she had identified these four essential values, some of the changes Greta knew she wanted to make were:

1. Spend more time with my loved ones.

2. Take the scuba diving class I've been eyeing for years.

3. Live in the country.

4. Study Italian.

5. Take better care of myself.

6. Allow joy to "count" or rule my decisions.

Now, using your four essential values, it's time to consider the life changes you need to make. Start this process by pulling out your list of four values and put them in front of you. Then, as you consider the following questions, make a list of all possible changes you could make to better express these values in your life.

- How does my life need to change in order to express these values?
- What do I need to add to my life?
- What do I need to remove?
- What major changes need to be considered?

Allow your mind to run wild without censoring your answers. Just make a list of all that occurs to you. Don't worry about how impossible or scary the changes might be; just be honest with yourself and write them down here:

1. _____   6. _____

2. _____   7. _____

3. _____   8. _____

4. _____   9. _____

5. _____   10. _____

Now, using your list of possible changes, narrow it down to three big life changes and list them here:

1. _____
2. _____
3. _____

As you look at these three life changes, ask yourself an important question:

Who would I have to be in order to make these changes?

Would you need to be someone who can make decisions even though it might hurt or disappoint others? How about someone who isn't afraid to express his or her power or who has a tremendous amount of courage? Maybe you'd need to have the emotional strength to say no or to value yourself enough to expect and accept only the best?

Pick up your journal and finish the following sentence:

In order to make these changes I would need to be someone who:

_____

Look back at your three life changes. These are the changes that will center your life around your values. Put this list aside. We'll use it again later in the program. If these changes seem challenging or insurmountable, don't worry. You have what it takes to step into the shoes of someone who can make it happen.

In the course of the next four chapters I'll take you through an "inner training program" that will help you build the necessary skills to lead an even more successful life. Since you've already begun creating a solid relationship with yourself, you've taken a giant step forward in the right direction. Now we'll focus on strategies that will allow you to express your power and I'll give you the language and skills you'll need to tell the truth with grace and love. Then we'll have a whole lot of fun building your courage muscles with exercises that challenge you to move out of your comfort zone. Finally, as your self-esteem increases you'll raise your standards so you can learn to pass up good for great.

As you continue to do the work outlined in this program, you'll find that the shyness or hesitation you may feel in exposing yourself and your gifts to others will slowly fade into an awakening power that will fuel your efforts to express your essential values. These values become a compelling reason to overcome your shyness, self-doubt, and fear of what others may think. Once you finish this part of the program you'll feel motivated and passionate about making these changes. Then we'll be ready to put this passion into action!

RESOURCES

Books

Sacred Contracts: Awakening Your Divine Potential by Carolyn Myss (Harmony Books, 2002)
   A wonderful book that will lead you to fulfill your divine potential.

Tuesdays with Morrie by Mitch Albom (Doubleday, 1997)
   A wonderful story to read while you consider your true values.

Coach U
www.coachu.com
800-48COACH
   Coach U offers a variety of personal and corporate coach training programs along with courses for the general public including the "Tru
Values Program." For more information on their corporate coach training programs visit: *www.ccui.com*.

Magazines

O, The Oprah Magazine
P. O. Box 7831
Red Oak, IA 51591
1-888-446-4438
www.oprah.com
   This magazine is a powerful tool for anyone committed to his or her
personal and spiritual development.

CHAPTER THREE

Stop Hiding Your Power

THROUGHOUT THE DAY I watched as Lilly, a bright and beautiful young woman, shared her thoughts during my daylong workshop on building self-esteem. Each time she raised her hand to speak, she preceded her comments with phrases like: "This may sound a little crazy . . ." or "I'm not sure this is right but. . . ." Her hesitation prior to responding seemed strange given that Lilly was clearly one of the smartest women in the room. When she answered a question or offered her thoughts on a topic, her responses were always well thought out and right on target. As I listened to her talk, I had a hunch that her level of depth and intelligence were the very reason why she used these preambles before she spoke.

At one point during the afternoon I stopped Lilly midsentence and brought this behavior to her attention. She smiled shyly and admitted that she was afraid of appearing to be a know-it-all. As we explored the source of her behavior further, it became obvious that Lilly *did* know a lot. The daughter of a midwestern family, she had excelled in school from the moment she entered kindergarten. Lilly was reading by the age of four, finished high school two years early, received a scholarship to an

Ivy League college, and was the only sibling to achieve an advanced degree.

Not only was Lilly considered bright among her family members, but among friends and colleagues too. Yet her gift of intelligence made Lilly feel like an outsider early in life. As her discomfort with being smarter than most of the people around her grew, she started downplaying her knowledge in order to fit in. Early on Lilly learned to hide her power with words.

WHAT IS REAL POWER?

Power is the energy that fuels our actions. Unlike the traditional patriarchal definition of "power over," or control, real power is the spiritual energy that comes from living with integrity, from aligning your thoughts, words, and actions with the deepest part of who you are—your soul. The heart of your personal and spiritual development is all about creating this alignment.

Most of us think of power as having the confidence, strength, and courage to do what we want with our lives. In reality these qualities emerge as a result of living with integrity. Just as a magnificent painting comes into its full glory through the convergence of space, creativity, and energy, so shall you come into your full power as you start to think, talk, and behave in ways that are congruent with your spiritual self.

As you continue to fulfill your Divine assignment by investing in your personal and spiritual development and listening more intently to your inner wisdom, you naturally begin to live a more congruent life. This forms a solid foundation for you to stand upon as you head in the direction of taking this inner work out into the world. As you continue doing the work to strengthen this foundation, you'll want to stop engaging in the habits that prevent you from letting the fullness of who you are shine through. You'll need to stop hiding your power.

WHY WE HIDE OUR POWER

For years I've watched bright and talented people think, speak, and act in ways that minimize their power. I've seen clients plagued by self-doubt hold themselves back from taking important steps toward their desired goals. I've listened to them continually put themselves down in spite of the talent they possess. I've watched countless people subconsciously sabotage their success by taking (or not taking) the necessary actions to fuel their dreams. There's nothing sadder than watching someone bursting with potential hold back his or her power in this way.

We hide our power for a number of reasons. For example, if you were raised by rules like "don't brag" or "don't get a big head," you may have learned that there are negative consequences to feeling confident or sure of yourself. If you had a parent who was angry and filled with rage, it may not have been safe for you to express yourself fully. Many of us have received messages that told us to be modest, humble, or understated. While these qualities may be virtuous, taken to an extreme it only serves to keep our God-given talents and gifts hidden from others.

Whatever your reason for hiding your power, what matters most is what you do *now* to change it. Now that you've begun to develop a stronger relationship with yourself, it's time to stop hiding your power so you can use it to build the emotional strength and confidence necessary to center your life around your values.

HOW DO YOU HIDE YOUR POWER?

In what ways do you put yourself down, hold yourself back, or discount your strengths and talents? Like Lilly, you might temper your conversations with words that downplay your intelligence. Or you may have a habit of putting yourself down or making fun of yourself in some way. Maybe you respond to compliments with an off-handed, self-effacing remark to deflect attention. As I've mentioned before, we've all learned to downplay our greatness and, in this chapter, I'd like to bring your awareness to how *you* may be getting in your own way.

To see how you might be hiding your power, read through the following statements and check those that are true for you:

1. _____ When a friend puts himself down, I join in by saying something like: "If you think that's bad, wait 'til you hear what I do."

2. _____ I procrastinate.

3. _____ I feel overwhelmed by my negative thinking.

4. _____ I often say "I'm sorry" even when I haven't done anything wrong.

5. _____ I downplay my looks by how I dress.

6. _____ I tend to focus on worst case scenarios.

7. _____ When making a request I tend to beat around the bush to be nice.

8. _____ My friends tell me that I have a tendency to diminish my talents.

9. _____ I spend more time focusing on my weaknesses than on my strengths.

10. _____ I agonize over taking risks, so I often end up playing it safe.

11. _____ In my work I charge (or accept) less than I'm worth.

12. _____ I precede my responses to questions with statements like "this may sound stupid but, . . . "

13. _____ I tend to socialize with people who have low standards.

14. _____ I worry about everything.

15. _____ I don't accept compliments easily.

Let's see how you did. Follow the guidelines below:

- If you answered yes to numbers 1, 4, 7, 8, and 12, you have a tendency to hide your power with words.

- If you answered yes to numbers 2, 5, 11, 13, and 15, you have a tendency to hide your power with actions (or inactions).

- If you answered yes to numbers 3, 6, 9, 10, and 14, you have a tendency to hide your power by how you think.

As you can see, the examples above fall into three categories:

- your thoughts—how you think
- your words—what you say
- your actions—what you do (or don't do)

The thoughts we think on a moment-by-moment basis have the most powerful influence over our lives. As you've already learned, thoughts are creative, and they become the springboard for your emotions, words, and actions. When you lend words to your thoughts by vocalizing them, you give them even more power. And as you act on those thoughts, your actions become your defining experience. Remember this: *Everything that occurs in your life is in direct connection to the thoughts you think, the words you speak, and the actions you take.* When your thoughts, words, and actions are congruent and aligned with your values, you exercise your greatest use of power.

As you'll hear me say many times over the course of our work together, *awareness is the first step toward change.* As you become aware of how you're hiding your power, your behavior will automatically start to shift. When your behavior changes, you'll feel better about yourself, you'll start making choices that command respect, and your level of confidence and self-esteem will begin to rise. Most important of all, you'll begin to make your most valuable contributions to others by sharing the full range of your talents and gifts.

As we consider each of the three areas, identify the ways in which you hide your power. Let's start with the most fundamental way of all—how you think.

WHAT ARE YOU THINKING?

We would *never* get away with speaking to others the way we speak to ourselves. At any given moment, most of us have a ticker tape of negative, critical messages streaming through our heads: "She's smarter than I am," "I'm not disciplined enough to do what I really want to do," or "I'm fat, ugly, or too old." As you consider how often you engage in this kind of thinking, remember this: *Your thoughts direct the course of your life.* What you consistently focus on plays a key role in what shows up in your physical world. If you keep your mind centered on negative thoughts, you start having negative experiences. It's a simple universal law. The most fundamental way to express your power is by using your mind wisely.

Most of us start beating ourselves up mentally early in life. When we are repeatedly directed, corrected, and criticized by our parents, teachers, schoolmates, friends, community members, and religious leaders we experience shame. In addition, when these acts take place in front of others, it compounds our shame, crippling our ability to express and use our power. For example, your parents, though well meaning, may have disciplined you in front of your siblings. A teacher may have reprimanded you in front of an entire class. Even the normal teasing and finger-pointing done by schoolmates can deepen the shame you feel. Soon we internalize these critical messages and, as a result, start monitoring our thoughts and behaviors with a critical eye. For example, my client Patrick still remembers being teased about his flabby stomach by students in his 5th grade gym class. To this day he still has to quiet the inner critic that berates him for not being in perfect shape.

These early experiences are influential in shaping our ability to express ourselves fully. Past events that made us feel humiliated or shamed rise up to interfere with our adult lives and our ability to use our talents and gifts confidently. For example, early in my coaching career I consulted with an outplacement firm, coaching men and women who had been laid off from their jobs. As part of my intake process, I'd ask each client to intuitively identify significant experiences that might affect their ability to present themselves with confidence and ease. I told them not to think too much, but to notice what experiences first came to mind. One out of every three clients referred to an early childhood memory of feeling embarrassed or shamed in front of classmates at school. The men and women who referred to these experiences seemed to be the most nervous about starting the job search process.

At first I was surprised to see this reoccurring theme, but as we continued to work together, the reason became clear. As these men and women set out to make major changes in their lives, they needed to feel confident and self-assured. Instead they felt vulnerable. This vulnerability triggered memories of feeling powerless and awakened a critical internal voice that began to question their talents and abilities. As a result it became difficult to muster the confidence to sell themselves during a job interview.

Later in my coaching practice I would see this theme reappear as my clients set out to take steps toward their most important goals. Clients wrestled with an "inner critic" that constantly minimized their strengths and power. For example, an extremely talented entrepreneur feared being accused of overstating his talents and abilities on his bio or resume, indicating a visit from the old "I'm a fraud" critic. Interestingly enough, the more talented and creative the person was, the stronger the voice of their inner critic.

I remember a vivid example of this while taking an improvisational acting class early in my career. Daena Giardella, a well-respected acting coach in the Boston area, had developed a way to form a dialogue with the inner critic using a process called "outtake." This process encouraged actors to step out of a scene and give voice to his or her inner critic. I found it to be a telling example of what goes on in the minds of people.

During one class, Daena asked a young man, a professional actor, to give an impromptu monologue. I sat waiting eagerly to hear his work, since his skits were always so funny and entertaining. In the middle of delivering an amazing monologue, he started stuttering and stammering. At that moment, Daena yelled, "Outtake!" I was stunned by what came out of this young man's mouth. In response to her direction, he immediately yelled out: "You suck! I can't believe how horrible you are! You call yourself an actor? These people are wondering why they've wasted their time coming here today. You can't act to save your life. You make me sick!"

As I listened to this actor rant and rave about his disgusting performance, I was surprised by how inaccurate his perception of himself had been. He offered a poignant example of how hard we can be on ourselves.

The Inner Critic

Our internalized, critical voices give birth to an inner critic that constantly reminds us of our faults and imperfections. From discussions I've had with clients and audience members it seems we all share the same inner voice. Your inner critic may use different words, but the intent and effect are always the same—to rob you of your confidence and power. If you allow these critical voices to take charge, you'll end up living a restricted, joyless life.

My public speaking career has given me a wonderful opportunity to work with my inner critic. Though I've given hundreds of presentations over the years, I often struggled with the
same fears and anxieties about public speaking that most people
have. While on stage I've wrestled with thoughts like "Are you
kidding? No one likes what you're saying" or "You're not inspiring or motivating enough." As every speaker knows, the
worst time to have your inner critic pipe up is *during* your presentation. The moment you give power to the stream of negative
thoughts by self-consciously analyzing what you're saying, you
lose connection with your audience. The end result is exactly
what you fear most—a less than desirable presentation.

I finally came to understand the source of my problem during a conversation with Debbie Ford, author of *The Dark Side of
the Light Chasers.* Debbie said something that helped to reduce
my anxiety dramatically. She said: "It's not the audience you're
worrying about when you give your presentation, it's what *you*
think that really concerns you. You're afraid to face your inner
critic when you get off the stage."

Debbie was right. As soon as I got off stage I immediately
began picking apart my presentation, thinking of all the things I
should or shouldn't have said and beating myself up for any mistakes I perceived myself as making. In all my years of speaking,
what I had been most afraid of were the criticisms *I* directed at
myself. Until I learned to stand by myself regardless of my performance, my inner critic would continue to erode my confidence, rob me of my joy, and prevent me from using my best
abilities.

Take Action! Monitor Your Power-Hiding Thoughts

How does your thinking affect your ability to use your power? To find out, monitor your thoughts for one day. Buy a small notebook (unless your journal is a manageable size) and put it by your bed. Once you wake up, start keeping track of your thoughts. Then take it with you and stop at random times throughout the day to notice what's going through your mind. As you do, jot it down. Please don't judge these thoughts; just become a witness to your inner dialogue and capture it on the page.

At the end of your day, go back and review what you've written. What percentage of your thoughts build you up, give you confidence, or support your well-being? What percentage brings you down or prevents you from fully expressing your power? Are there any themes? For example, do you beat yourself up about your physical appearance, your performance at work, or the quality of your parenting? If you're like most people, you'll probably notice that a high percentage of your thoughts are power-stealing, self-defeating ones. You may have thoughts like:

> You always make mistakes.
>
> Why start? You never follow through with what you say you're going to do anyway.
>
> That was such a stupid thing to say.
>
> You're not good enough.
>
> You don't have what it takes to succeed.
>
> You're not a good enough role model for your son.

No one cares what you have to say.

You're such a lazy person.

Keep your mouth shut; you'll only look foolish.

You don't deserve it.

You're not qualified.

Don't bother anyone with your needs.

No matter how hard you try you'll never win.

You'll look like you're smarter than the others.

Someone else can do it better.

Take Action! List Your Power-Hiding Thoughts

Now it's your turn. Review your notebook or journal and make a list of your ten most common critical thoughts:

1. _____   6. _____

2. _____   7. _____

3. _____   8. _____

4. _____   9. _____

5. _____   10. _____

Becoming aware of how these thoughts interfere with your ability to feel confident and empowered will make a big difference. Share your list and journal entries with your partner or Life Makeover Group. You might be surprised by what you hear. When I ask audiences to write down and share the common negative messages they receive from their inner critic, they're always surprised at how similar the voices are to each other. You'd swear we all belong to the same family!

_____

WATCH WHAT YOU SAY

The thoughts we think often translate into the words we speak, and the words we choose (and use) play an important role in how we increase or decrease our confidence and self-esteem. Do the words you use command respect and attention, or do they minimize your power and sense of self-worth?

There are many words and phrases that we use unconsciously to diminish or minimize our power. For example, I often hear people joking around about themselves by using phrases like "I'm so stupid" or "I'm such an idiot." When I hear these phrases I cringe knowing that our words affect the way we feel about ourselves and how others perceive us. Let's look at some examples.

"I think"

Courtney had a bad habit of using the phrase "I think." It showed up in almost every coaching conversation. When I asked her about a project she completed at work, she responded, "I think I did a good job." When I suggested that she take more of a leadership role in her community, she'd say: "I think I can handle running that meeting." This phrase even showed up often in her personal life. When a friend invited her to dinner, she'd accept the invitation by saying something like "I think I can make it to your house next week."

When clients temper their statements with "I think" I challenge them by asking: "Do you think, or do you _know?_" More often than not, the answer is "I know." It just feels safer to say "I think." Learning to state the truth with conviction raises your confidence and self-esteem. For example, saying "I know I did a great job" instead of "I think I did a great job" is a much more powerful declaration. When we take a bold stance and own our success, we stop hiding our power.

"I'll try"

The phrase "I'll try" is another good example of how we hide our power. My friend Stephen challenged me to stop using the word "try" when I promised to *try* and arrange a time for us to get together. He said: "Are you going to try or are you going to set a date? The word try is just a way to put off making a decision. Either you want to get together or you don't." Though I was annoyed at first (a good indication that he was right), Stephen's comment made me think. Did I really want to get together or was I creating a loophole in case I changed my mind?

Try is a hedge word, a convenient way to ride the fence. Of course there are times when we're undecided and in process with something, but in these cases it's much more powerful to say something like "I'm not sure yet" or "I'm not ready to decide." Rather than trying to keep expectations low or buying yourself time, take a more powerful position. Now when I catch myself using the word "try," I ask myself: "What's the truth?" From there a simple yes, no, or maybe will suffice.

"I'm sorry"

How often do you apologize for something you didn't do? When my friend Allison decided to learn how to play tennis, she learned an important lesson about apologizing. During her first class, she constantly apologized for not hitting the ball back over the net to her instructor. After more than twenty apologies her tennis instructor finally turned to her and said: "Why are you apologizing for not doing something you haven't learned how to do yet? Don't you know that by saying you're sorry you keep putting yourself in the one-down position? From that point of view you're going to have a tough time capturing enough confidence and skill to play this game."

Suddenly Allison realized the link between this habit and her power. Apologizing for things that she couldn't control was not only draining her energy but interfering with her ability to develop the skills that would allow her to master the game.

These are just a few examples of the words or phrases we use to hide our power. Let's look at what you say.

Take Action! Identify Your Power-Hiding Language

What words or phrases do *you* use? Do you joke around about being a klutz? Do you lower the expectations of others when answering a question by starting with something like "I could be wrong, but . . . ? " Now I'd like you to identify the words or phrases that you use to hide your power. Grab your journal, a pen, and some quiet time alone in a comfortable spot to consider these questions:

1. What do you say that diminishes who you are?
2. What words do you use to lower the expectations of others?
3. Do you put yourself down? If so, how?

Once you've answered the questions, ask three close friends or family members for help in finding more examples. Choose people you can trust to tell you the truth without judgment or criticism. You might be surprised at how perceptive your loved ones are about the way you hide your power. List five examples here:

Power-Hiding Language:

1. _____
2. _____
3. _____
4. _____
5. _____

_____

WHAT ARE YOU DOING (OR NOT DOING)?

Now that we've looked at some of the ways your thoughts and words allow you to hide your power, let's look at some of your behaviors. Most of us have adopted habits that fuel our negative thinking. These actions can run the gamut from overeating and smoking to embellishing the truth when telling a story. Anything you do that makes you feel bad about yourself diminishes your power.

In doing research for this book, I asked several people to share the actions they take that hide their power. Here's what they had to say:

> I tell little white lies.
>
> I procrastinate.
>
> I break the promises I make to myself.
>
> I'm a perfectionist.

I don't ask for what I want directly.

I shut down and remain silent when my husband and I disagree.

I pretend not to know an answer when asked a question to make someone else feel smarter.

I don't speak up for myself when something bothers me.

I stay at a job I can't stand.

I ask questions I already know the answers to.

I don't charge enough for my services.

I let others make decisions for me.

I deflect compliments.

I stay so busy that I never have the time or energy to do what I want to do.

I keep ignoring my health.

When faced with conflict, I always give in.

I don't ask for help.

What do you do (or not do) that hides your power? There are a variety of actions that hide our power. Some of them have come as a surprise to both my clients and me.

My client Gabriella is a multitalented woman. Not only is she very attractive and personable, she's extremely successful in her work as an events director for a hotel. Gabriella had a hard time coming up with actions that hid her power, so I asked her to check in with a work colleague whom she trusted. This colleague told Gabriella that though she had exceptional communication skills when dealing with people one-on-one, she had a strange habit of giggling and talking like a little girl during meetings when speaking in front of others.

I've seen similar behavior with women in executive positions who diminish their power by deferring to their male colleagues or downplaying their strengths and knowledge when in the company of male executives.

Once this behavior was called to her attention, Gabriella realized that this nervous habit was her way of dealing with the discomfort she felt at being the center of attention. While one part of Gabriella loved being in the limelight, another part felt uncomfortable with that desire. Whenever she found herself in a situation where she actually needed to project powerfully, the part of her that felt uncomfortable would express itself with giggles and a little girl voice.

Another way we hide our power is by the image we present to others. Although most of us would like to believe that we will be accepted for who we are and not what we look like, the truth is that your image has a profound effect on how powerful you feel and on how powerful you appear to others.

Do you know how your image is affecting your success? Do you hide your power by not allowing your outside image to be congruent with who you are on the inside? Image can be the determining factor in many situations, whether you know it or not. Ginger Burr, a top image expert in the Boston area, has had plenty of opportunities to see the powerful influence image has on the lives of her clients. The following story from Ginger shows what happens when our inner self is brought into direct alignment with our external image.

Madeline, a gifted interior designer who provides high-end, professional, corporate design work, was having trouble building her business. She decided to meet with Ginger about her image after five potential clients all had similar reactions when looking at her portfolio. Each time she met with a potential client, their initial response was always the same: "*You* did this?" The element of surprise in his or her voice made Madeline feel like a fraud, as if the inference was that someone more talented and professional had actually done the design work. She said that each time she heard this reaction, she felt as though who they saw in her and what they saw in her work were incongruent.

Madeline had a bohemian sense of style and dressed in what she called "earthy crunchy" comfortable clothes that made her feel totally at ease. When Ginger met with Madeline, she could see that her style of clothing was relaxed and casual, unlike her portfolio, which was more polished and professional. Madeline complained of not wanting to change her style to meet someone else's expectations. She wanted people to accept her the way she really was. But she could no longer deny the reality that her image might have been affecting her business. Ginger put it to the test.

Ginger's work is geared toward helping her clients express their natural beauty and style in a way that feels right. Keeping Madeline's desire for comfort and ease in mind, Ginger recommended that she purchase a few soft, comfortable pantsuits in her favorite colors (colors that enhanced her features and skin tone). She also had her use accessories that accentuated her love of a more bohemian style. When they were finished Madeline just looked like a more upbeat, contemporary version of herself.

Madeline was stunned by the results. Not once did she hear someone say "*You* did that?" Instead, new potential clients immediately complimented her work. Feeling empowered, Madeline's image also improved her approach with new clients. She felt much more confident, and it showed. At the end of the year, Madeline's sales increased by 30 percent!

Whether you're a man or a woman, see if your image might need to be enhanced to allow your power to shine through. Complete the following quiz with yes or no answers.

____ All of my clothing is in good repair.

____ I fit into everything in my wardrobe—nothing is too big or too small.

____ I know what colors I look best in and wear those colors exclusively.

____ I know what styles flatter my body type and never settle for anything less.

____ I am always open to new ideas about what looks good on me.

____ I have a makeup routine that I like and that enhances my best features.

____ My nails and eyebrows are always well groomed.

____ I feel good about my smile.

____ I have a hairstyle and color that are contemporary and flattering.

____ My shoes are well cared for.

____ I always look professional and well put together at work (even on "casual day").

____ I have a good "business casual" wardrobe—separate from my weekend clothing.

____ I always choose a wardrobe that is congruent with my personality and that reflects who I am at a deeper level.

Don't underestimate the power of image in helping you to express more of who you really are. By recommending that you take your image seriously I'm not suggesting that you run out and buy designer label clothing. Designer labels do not express power; a congruency between who you are and how you dress does.

WHAT AREN'T YOU DOING?

Sometimes the actions we don't take hide our power. For example, my client Ryan had a problem with procrastination. Ryan is an artist who does the most amazing watercolor paintings, and yet he could not get his art business off the ground. As we explored his office, the reason was obvious. His studio was filled with junk; he often forgot appointments; and although three local galleries had contacted him about his work, he still hadn't returned their calls. The strange thing was that the rest of Ryan's life ran smoothly. His apartment was neat and orderly; he had several friends who loved hanging out with him and his personal life seemed to be in good shape.

On some level Ryan knew that he was a very talented artist—more talented than most. As we explored his habit of procrastination at work he admitted that it was a shield that hid his power. Although Ryan said he was afraid to put his art out into the world for fear of having his work scrutinized, I knew it was more than that. Ryan was afraid of being able to effectively handle the success that would likely come his way. This is a common problem with highly talented people who feel burdened by their talent and who procrastinate. They feel as though they can't handle the responsibility they already have, so more success feels overwhelming. Rather than get the help they need, they just stay stuck.

Emily had a different problem. One of the ways she hid her power was by being indirect about what she wanted and needed. At work, when coworkers invited her to lunch, rather than say directly which restaurant she preferred, she'd ask a question like "Has anyone been to the new restaurant on the corner?" At home with her husband she constantly complained about having to do more of the household chores rather than ask directly for more help. Emily had picked up this habit from her mom who, for years, was never able to say what she needed directly. Instead she went through life acting like a powerless victim at the mercy of everyone else's needs.

Brooke hid her power by talking too much. It wasn't until she came across a bold new friend who had the courage to tell her the truth that she realized how this habit was getting in her way. Brooke admitted that over the years people had made comments and little jokes about how much she talked, but she never took them seriously. Now she was paying attention. Brooke was lucky to have been given this information. Unfortunately, most people who talk too much never get the benefit of the truth; instead people simply avoid them!

There are many other actions that hide our power. For example, we might stay so busy that we never get to spend our time and energy on our top priorities. Do you have a habit of always giving in to the needs of others? Or maybe you deflect compliments whenever they come your way. What do you do (or not do) to hide your power?

Take Action! Identify Your Power-Hiding Actions/Inactions

Look back over the personal examples on pages 94–95 and identify five ways that you hide your power by what you do or don't do. If you're not sure, ask a trusted friend, your partner, or members of your Life Makeover Group for help in identifying some of your patterns. You might even keep a log in your journal during the next week, of those moments when you notice yourself doing something that hides your power.

List your five examples here:

1. _____
2. _____
3. _____
4. _____
5. _____

RECLAIM YOUR POWER

Now that you have a good idea of how you hide your power there's a good chance that you've already begun to shift your behavior. Awareness is the first step. You've probably even become a bit self-conscious about your self-defeating thoughts, words, and actions. You can relax in knowing that as soon as you start to make specific changes, even little ones, you'll begin to feel more confident and empowered. Let's start by retraining your mind.

Retrain Your Mind

Earlier in this program I said that the thoughts you think have the most powerful influence over the quality of your life. You've already begun to take more control of your mind by incorporating meditation into your daily life, as well as by doing simple exercises to claim ownership of your creative power to shape your life. Now I'd like to help you take this work further.

Take Action! Shift Your Thinking

Years ago I remember hearing a story about Mark Victor Hansen, one of the creators of the *Chicken Soup for the Soul* series. Mark would write down his goals in detail on two index cards and keep one in his wallet and one on his bathroom mirror to help him focus on his goals. When getting ready to start the day, or when removing money from his wallet, he would visualize himself as having already achieved his goal as soon as he spotted the card. When I heard about his technique I decided to use it in a different way.

I bought a package of little red heart stickers and placed them at various spots in my home—on the refrigerator door, by the kitchen sink, on the bathroom mirror, or anywhere else that would cause me to see them on a regular basis. Each time I came in contact with a heart I stopped to check in with my thoughts to be sure that they were supporting my emotional well-being. This constructive method, albeit simple, helped to train my mind to follow my heart's direction.

My friend Charles Poliquin, a strength coach who trains professional athletes, has a similar approach. When he helps clients get into winning shape he has them imagine their body at its optimum fitness level. When there, he then has them create an affirmation to support this vision. Once his clients have developed a firm vision of their success, Charles instructs them to purchase a package of at least five hundred toothpicks. The clients then use these toothpicks by shifting them one at a time from one pocket to another while repeating their affirmation and visualizing their fitness goal. When a client has gone through one whole package, he has them repeat the process one more time. Charles has learned from experience that it takes one thousand reps to set the vision firmly in the client's mind.

Retraining your mind ensures that you use your power wisely. To determine the quality of your thoughts you need only pay attention to your emotions. *Your feelings always follow your thought patterns.* For example, I've learned to stop and ask myself the following question the moment I feel a sense of disharmony:

Does this way of thinking serve me?

If my way of thinking does *not* support my emotional health, I immediately shift my thoughts to something that does. For example, I might focus on a specific word like "balance," or "love," or I might use a phrase like "move on," or "all is well." Rather than trying to figure out why I'm not feeling well, I simply focus my energy on raising my thoughts to a level of health and well-being that serves me. Long ago I learned an important lesson about dealing with negativity from a meditation teacher. She used the following analogy: "Imagine your mind as a beautiful antique cup. When this cup is filled with negative thoughts, trying to remove them will waste precious energy and only give them more power. Instead, put your energy into filling the cup with positive thoughts so that the negativity just spills out." So, when I'm feeling frustrated, down, or filled with self-doubt, I have three or four favorite books that I turn to when I want a dose of inspiration or power-inducing thoughts!

Decide on a daily practice that you'll use to retrain your mind. Purchase a package of stickers or toothpicks to get you started. As simple as this exercise may sound, those who do it can attest to how effective it is. Keep a couple of your favorite books nearby too. The goal is to take charge of your mind!

Take Action! Make Peace with Your Inner Critic

The next step in retraining your mind is to make peace with your inner critic. There are a couple of effective ways to actually use the energy and wisdom of your inner critic to your advantage. For example, years ago, while taking a workshop with Henriette Klauser, author of *Writing on Both Sides of the Brain,* I learned an important lesson about dealing with my inner critic. During a writing exercise Henriette asked us to engage in a written dialogue with our inner critic as soon as we came in contact with its noise. She suggested that we use the following questions to open a dialogue:

- What are you afraid of?
- What can you teach me?

As soon as I began to write I could feel my inner critic start in with "you're going to do this exercise wrong" or "you need a lot of work on your writing." I immediately stopped and asked my inner critic what it was trying to teach me. After several paragraphs of more noise, it finally said, "I'm trying to protect you from writing something foolish." As I continued the dialogue I could see that I simply needed to give voice to the vulnerable part of myself that was afraid. As I listened with compassion, I was able to continue a dialogue that felt more informative and less abusive.

Over the years, as I've used this and other similar techniques, I've learned that as critical as that voice inside us seems, it's usually trying to share important information. To make peace you need only listen to its wisdom. Nine times out of ten the underlying message of your inner critic is based in fear and when you open a dialogue it's as if you put your arm around your critic and include it in your creative process. As you do you'll find that it starts to assist you rather than work against you.

Take Action! Develop an Inner Ally

Daena Giardella, the improvisational acting coach I mentioned earlier in this chapter, has another great way of working with the inner critic. She recommends that her students create an "inner ally." The inner ally is a potent antidote to the inner critic. It's like an internal friend whose voice becomes so well-developed that it quiets the inner critic down.

To develop your inner ally start by making a list of statements that support you. Begin this exercise by identifying the qualities of character that you are most proud of and that support the use of your power. Then, put these qualities into "you" statements. For example, one client said she was gracious, kind, strong, and courageous. From there she created several direct messages to herself using these qualities. She wrote: "You are a

gracious and kind woman" and "You are a strong and courageous soul." Once she had created several statements in her
journal, she then entered them into her computer and printed
them out using a large-sized font. It was important for her to see
these statements every day in an effort to "install" the voice of
her inner ally securely in her mind.

Try it right now. Identify five of your best qualities and list
them here:

1. _____

2. _____

3. _____

4. _____

5. _____

Now, using these qualities, create five "you" statements that will
remind you of how powerful you are:

1. _____

2. _____

3. _____

4. _____

5. _____

You can use this information to support you in many ways. For
example, let's imagine that you are preparing for a job interview
and you're really nervous. You know that you're a great computer programmer with stellar skills, but in previous interviews
you've often been overcome with fear, which impeded your
ability to speak confidently about your experience. Feeling vul-

nerable, your inner critic kicks in with its usual negative messages: "You always ramble on and on and never get to the point" and "No one would want to hire you." But rather than give into this power-diminishing voice, you give voice to your inner ally by repeating your statements out loud on your way to the interview: "You are a smart and highly skilled programmer" or "You are an intelligent person who knows exactly what to say." You might want to record these positive statements on a tape and listen to them on the way to the interview.

The more you rely on your inner ally, the stronger and more able you are to face any fearful circumstance. If you have trouble coming up with language for your inner ally, ask your partner or Life Makeover Group members for help. Ask someone in your group to act as your inner ally by speaking to you in a competent, powerful voice about your best qualities. Be sure to write down these statements so you can begin to develop the script that you'll need to help create your own inner ally.

There are other practical reminders you can use to bolster the voice of your inner ally. They include:

- Draw, paint, or sculpt an image of your inner ally and keep it in view.

- Purchase some type of symbol or statue that represents your inner ally (I use a statue of Quan Yin, the goddess of compassion and mercy).

- Write a letter in your journal to yourself from your inner ally (book mark the page!).

- Give your inner ally a name _____.

- Keep a photo of yourself feeling confident and strong in a place where you'll see it often.

As I was finishing up this section, I happened to speak with my friend SARK, an experienced writer who has written more than eleven books of her own, the latest of which is called *Prosperity Pie.* I asked SARK how she handles her inner critic. This is what she said: "Well, I have several. Some inner critics I banish and some I reassign. For example, I have reassigned the inner critic that tells me that I need to take care of everyone to be of value, to Afghanistan. She's taking care of refugees right now while I'm focused on my writing."

Are there some inner critics you need to banish or reassign? Which ones? Who are they?

_____

_____

_____

Watch Your Words

Now that you're taking better control of your thoughts, it's time to talk about the importance of shifting your language.

Take Action! Revise Your Vocabulary

This week, pay attention to how often you use words that undermine your power. Refer back to the list you created earlier on page 94 and check out the list below for some ideas on how to shift your language:

Old Words	New Words
"I think"	"I know"
"I'll try"	"I will"

"Maybe"	"Definitely"
"I'm not sure"	"I'm positive"
"I guess"	"I'll confirm that"
"I'm sorry"	"I'm confident"
"I'm so stupid"	"I need a break"
"It doesn't matter"	"Here's what I want"
"We'll see"	"I will"

Now, list your three old words or phrases along with the new words or phrases that you'll replace them with here:

Old   *New*

1. _____   1. _____

2. _____   2. _____

3. _____   3. _____

Ask your partner or someone from your Life Makeover Group for help in coming up with new words or phrases that are more empowering. When you do, there's a great little technique you can use to help break the habit of using language that hides your power. You'll need a partner with whom you spend a lot of time and who you trust to have your best interest at heart. Ask that person to gently tap you on the shoulder when you use a word or phrase that you'd like to change. Let this gentle tap simply remind you to stop and shift your language. When I have clients use this technique with a loved one, it usually takes about two weeks for the reminder to stick.

Act in a New Way

Now here's the last step. It's time to change the behaviors that hide your power. For example, you might decide to stop deflecting compliments. When we deflect compliments it's usually because we don't want someone else to feel inferior, so we downplay ourselves just to make the other person feel comfortable. For example, when someone says "You look great today; I love your suit," you might seek to level the playing field by saying "This old suit? I've had it for years. You're the one who looks great!"

My mom and I helped each other to change this behavior by using a little game. Each of us had a hard time accepting compliments, so we decided to simply use the phrase "thank you" as a reminder to graciously accept the gift that someone offered. Anytime one of us heard the other begin to deflect, we simply smiled and said "Just say thank you."

Early in our relationship my husband, Michael, and I had a bad habit of being indirect with each other when we were deciding on activities to do together. To remedy the problem, we began using a ten-point scale to shift our behavior from being wishy-washy and indirect to direct. When Michael asks "Do you want to go to the movies tonight?" I either say yes when I know for sure, or I tell him on a scale of 1 to 10 whether I feel like going—and vice versa. We've both agreed to be honest about our number.

This ten-point scale also helps with difficult choices like when one of us wants to do something that the other may not want to do. For example, if Michael asks me to attend a social event and I say no, he registers his desire for me to join him using this scale. In other words, he knows that if he's at nine or ten in terms of how strongly he wants me to go, I'll agree to join him. Not only has this simple system allowed us to directly communicate our needs, it's prevented a lot of arguments.

Take Action! Eliminate Your Power-Hiding Actions/Inactions

What will you do (or not do) to stop hiding your power? When you shift your behavior from power-diminishing actions to power-enhancing ones, there's a good chance that you'll feel a bit uncomfortable. It's perfectly fine to "fake it" in the beginning. Before you know it, you'll fit into your cloak of power just fine. Here are some questions to consider:

What do you need to start doing?

What do you need to stop doing?

What actions will you shift?

Do you need to stop talking too much?

Do you need to update your image?

Do you need to receive compliments with grace and ease?

Do you need to start having and sharing your opinions?

Do you need to stop procrastinating?

Is there an action you need to take to respect yourself more?

Do you need to admit when you don't know something?

Do you need to start asking directly for what you want or need?

The five things I need to do differently are:

1. _____

2. _____

3. _____

4. _____

5. _____

It's only as you become conscious of how your actions (or inactions) are robbing you of your power that you can begin to make a shift—awareness is the first step. Challenge yourself to change the way you behave in one small way each day. For example, if you're used to allowing your husband to select the movie you'll see, pick out the movie yourself. If your office is overflowing with clutter, spend 10 minutes a day getting it organized. Find a quiet place to plan your day. Take one hour a day to do exactly what you want to do. Be patient and compassionate with yourself—these changes won't happen over night.

Take Action! Put Your Power Tools Together

Before we finish this chapter, let's create an action plan that will inspire you to change your thoughts, words and actions. Fill in the following information:

To retrain my mind I will:

_____

I will develop and strengthen the voice of my inner ally by doing the following three things:

1. _____

2. _____

3. _____

I will replace the following words or phrases with new, empowering ones:

Old Word/Phrase   New Word/Phrase

_____   _____

_____   _____

_____   _____

_____   _____

I will stop doing:

_____

_____

I will start doing:

_____

_____

RESOURCES

Books

Power Through Constructive Thinking by Emmet Fox (Harper, San Francisco, 1989)
When I want to reorient my thinking in the right direction, I pick up this book. Filled with practical wisdom, it's one of my favorites.

Find and Use Your Inner Power by Emmet Fox (Harper, San Francisco, 1992)
This book is a series of short essays on the power of thought to direct the course of your life.

Fashion Secrets Mother Never Taught You by Ginger Burr (Total Image Consultants, 1999)
Fashion Secrets Mother Never Taught You is a fashion resource designed to guide women through the process of creating a polished and professional look that saves them time and money and takes the guesswork out of getting dressed in the morning!

Prosperity Pie: How to Relax About Money and Everything Else by SARK (Fireside, 2002)
When you're fed up with worrying about money and you want some peace of mind, pick up this book!

Writing on Both Sides of the Brain by Henriette Anne Klauser (Harper San Francisco, 1987)
A great book for writers who want to handle their inner critic.

Websites

www.beliefnet.org
This is a terrific website that provides a wealth of inspiration and information on topics that include spirituality, religion, family, morality, community, and more.

www.totalimageconsultants.com
This website offers a variety of information on image, fashion, makeup, and skincare to help you express your inner values through your outer image.

www.campsark.com
SARK'S website has a variety of tools to help you reconnect with your creative power.

www.daenagiardella.com
Daena offers live performances, "improvisation for life" coaching, and improvisational acting workshops on the East and West Coasts.

CHAPTER FOUR

Stand Up for Yourself

N
OW THAT YOU'VE BEGUN to reclaim your power, it's important that you build on that foundation by becoming your own greatest ally and advocate. This means developing the tools you'll need to stand up for yourself. As you learned in the previous chapter, power is the spiritual energy that fuels your efforts to live an authentic, purposeful life. You saw that by allowing your mind to focus on self-defeating thoughts or by using words and actions that lower your self-esteem, you hide your power. There is another way to lose power—by giving it away to others.

When you allow others to rob you of time, energy, or peace of mind, you essentially give your power away. For example, if you avoid conflict by not asking directly for what you want, or neglect to set boundaries with someone who steals your energy, you put other people in charge of your life. And, as you allow others to call the shots, you send a message to yourself (and others) that you are not worthy of having your needs met.

One morning while taking a shower, my friend Caroline noticed two small moles on her chest that looked suspicious. After several days of trying to convince herself that nothing was wrong, she gave in and made an appointment with her dermatologist. One week later, feeling anxious, she arrived early for her appointment and was shown to an examining room.

Caroline was told to change into a scant gown and that the doctor would be with her shortly. As she sat on the table waiting for the doctor to come in, her nervousness increased. After 45 minutes, Caroline grew frustrated and even more anxious. She was tempted to get dressed and visit the reception area to find out what was taking the doctor so long, but not wanting to appear pushy, she decided to sit patiently and wait.

Fifteen minutes later, her doctor walked in with an intern and asked Caroline if it would be all right if his intern observed the examination. Without missing a beat, Caroline immediately said, "That's okay," and the examination began. Inside she was furious. She thought to herself: "I can't believe I have to sit here waiting for an hour and then be made to feel vulnerable while a stranger watches my chest being examined! This is so humiliating and I feel so embarrassed. How could my doctor be so insensitive?" Twenty minutes later, when Caroline left the office with a clean bill of health, she was still fuming. But the focus of her anger had shifted. She was furious with herself for not having said something to her doctor.

Later that afternoon, Caroline called to tell me what had happened. When I asked her why she didn't speak up, she simply said, "I don't know, I felt embarrassed and just couldn't seem to find my voice." From there she proceeded to beat herself up by comparing this event to all the other times when she had neglected to stand up for herself in the past.

I'm sure you've had your own share of experiences that left you feeling angry with yourself for not speaking up or for agreeing to do something that you later regretted. For example, maybe you couldn't bring yourself to speak up to a friend who criticized your parenting style or to a stranger who cut you off in line at the post office. You might have agreed to help a friend with her computer on a night when you really would have preferred staying at home with your family. Or maybe you've been unable to request a long-awaited raise at work, or to set a boundary with a friend who constantly complains about the drama in her life.

For most of us, putting the needs of others before our own is an unconscious habit we've carried with us since childhood. Hungry for love and approval, it becomes second nature to automatically say yes without considering the consequences. It's only human to want to be well-liked, appreciated, and valued. But when we become full-fledged people-pleasers who spend more time worrying about everyone but ourselves, we get into trouble. We become martyrs, or at best, chronically resentful, and we're not much fun to be around. My client Theresa was a good example of someone who was stuck in the martyr role.

Theresa was known for being the mom in the neighborhood whom everyone could count on. If someone needed a baby-sitter, they called Theresa. If kids needed to be car-pooled, you could usually find at least four in her car. When it came time to celebrate a birthday, Theresa always stepped in to throw the party. When her adult children left home and got into trouble, they always called mom to bail them out. After years of playing the hero, Theresa was burned out and bitter.

During every one of our initial conversations, Theresa complained about her kids' problems, and about the friends who never initiated contact with her. She said she felt resentful and lonely and wished that people appreciated her more. Instead, she said, they only turned to her when they needed something. I was beginning to understand why.

Sometimes people-pleasing is just a familiar jacket that we put on in childhood and wear into adulthood. As one of five children, Theresa learned to please people early in life to get attention. She helped out at home, worked hard to get good grades, and was the first person to support her friends when they were in need. As an adult, this role wasn't working anymore. Her friends were tired of "feeling" her resentment and hearing her complain about her kids. In one of our coaching calls, while talking to Theresa about taking responsibility for the situation she had created, I challenged her to stop being a martyr and take on a new, more empowering role. Theresa agreed that she needed to stop giving her power away to others by setting better limits on what she would and would not do. She was ready to shed her martyr role and take her power back.

If people-pleasing isn't a familiar role, there may be other reasons why you don't stand up for yourself. For example, if you project your fear of conflict onto someone else, it might keep you from telling the truth. Or you may want to avoid the inevitable uneasiness that comes with differing points of view. Maybe you suffer from "conflict phobia"—an aversion to conflict of any kind.

CONFLICT PHOBIA

Does the phrase "go along to get along" sound like your motto in life? Have you ever been able to discuss a difference of opinion comfortably with someone without feeling your heart rate soar and your palms sweat? Perhaps you're conflict phobic. See if you identify with any of the following statements:

- You tolerate bad behavior from others and often fantasize about what you should have said after an altercation.

- You feel sick to your stomach at the mere thought of having to stand up for yourself.

- You immediately feel "charged up," as though electricity were coursing through your veins, when faced with conflict.

- Rather than address any kind of conflict, you turn to food, alcohol, cigarettes, work, house cleaning, or television to numb your anxious feelings.

- You rationalize bad behavior and try to downplay your hurt rather than confront someone who treated you poorly.

- You replay a negative exchange over and over in your mind trying to make sense out of someone else's inappropriate behavior.

- You passively apologize or agree rather than speak your truth.

If you see yourself in any of the above statements, it may be an indication that you give your power away by avoiding conflict or by not speaking up for what you want. Conflict phobia has its roots in early childhood based on how friction and disharmony were handled in your home. Did your parents resort to yelling, belittling, or violence? Were you emotionally or physically abandoned after an outburst or argument? Could you express yourself freely without fear of harmful repercussions? Our fear of conflict starts at home. If you saw your parents handle day-to-day problems with yelling, physical violence, or shaming behavior, it's only natural that you'll have a tough time with conflict later in life.

While attending a family reunion on Cape Cod, I witnessed a chilling example of how messages about handling conflict are passed down from parent to child. One night, while getting ready for dinner, I overheard a man in the next room yelling at his young son. The boy, who must have been about four years old, was crying loudly. While the boy was crying his father was yelling at him to stop. The more he sobbed, the more his father yelled. I was shocked by what I heard the father saying: "If you don't stop it, Jack, I'm going to give you away! I'm sick and tired of you crying all the time. Stop it right now or else." As this man yelled, the boy just cried harder, until his father took a dramatic step. He opened his front door, put his young child outside, and slammed the door shut!

Having learned not to incite a parent further by attacking their actions, I walked over to ask the man if he needed help. But before I reached the door, he immediately yanked the child back inside. I stood outside the door stunned by what I had seen, and finally, feeling rattled, I walked away. It was such a blatant illustration of how parents teach children about conflict through their own reactions to distress. While I was sure this man's anger and frustration had more to do with other circumstances, I knew that his overreaction and rage would have a direct impact on how this little boy responded to conflict in the future.

The mishandling of conflict in your family need not be as dramatic as the example above to create a fear of conflict. My client Connie had a mom who gave her the silent treatment whenever she was upset with her daughter's behavior. Although

Connie was never yelled at or physically harmed, her mother's silence left Connie feeling emotionally abandoned and seriously wounded. Each time her mother shut down, Connie was terrified by the thought that she may never speak to her again. As she reached adulthood, Connie avoided conflict at all costs by doing the very thing her mother did, when faced with disharmony—she shut down and remained silent.

Often our fear of conflict requires therapeutic intervention. For example, if you are unable to follow the advice in this chapter, or if your attempts to stand up for yourself with a toxic family member (the most challenging of all) fail, it may be an indication that there is deeper work to be done. Because our personal history has such a strong effect on our ability to stand up for ourselves as adults, it may be necessary to heal past emotional issues before taking any action. For example, if violence was a part of your past, you may have such a strong reaction to any kind of conflict that you become immobilized by your fear. In this case, the idea of asking your boss for a raise may very well bring up feelings of terror. If the emotional charge around a situation is out of proportion, no amount of planning will make facing conflict bearable. You need to do the emotional healing work first.

This is important. Too often I'm approached privately by audience members who are struggling with a toxic person. This person is usually a demanding or highly critical family member. After trying everything under the sun to tell the truth and heal the relationship (which usually means twisting themselves into a pretzel to make the other person happy), he or she never finds a resolution. They're usually desperate for a new strategy to try and make the relationship work.

First of all it's important to note that if you cannot tell the truth and be yourself with someone, it's not a relationship; it's an arrangement. When you have difficulty setting boundaries with a toxic person in your life, it may be that you need the support of a good therapist, not a new method of relating.

One of the main reasons we avoid having difficult conversations is because we lack the language for resolution. Most of us have never been taught how to tell the truth with grace and love. Instead we usually wait until we're so charged up, resentful, or angry before we address an issue. Then, brimming with strong emotions, we end up projecting our anger or frustration onto the other person and, as a result, rarely get the resolution we desire. In fact, we only make matters worse.

The costs of not standing up for yourself are significant. Each time you neglect to ask for what you need, or to confront someone who treats you poorly, you chip away at your confidence and self-esteem. Your emotional well-being suffers as you stuff your feelings inside and beat yourself up for what you should have said or done. And when you keep putting off a difficult conversation, as you'll see in Robin's case, you just increase the chances of it happening over and over again.

My friend Robin became aware of the cost of not standing up for herself after getting sick on a week-long retreat with friends. Her roommate had invited along a woman named Adrienne who was known for making sarcastic remarks. Throughout the early part of the week Adrienne poked fun at Robin's clothes and hair. When Robin chose to let this "teasing" pass, Adrienne could see that she was an easy target and kept up the jokes and sarcastic comments. Although Robin felt annoyed by these comments, she didn't want to make a big deal out of what she considered to be stupid, snide remarks, so she decided to let it go. Or so she thought.

Later in the week Robin started to feel physically ill. She felt sick to her stomach and feared that she might be coming down with the flu. When I asked Robin whether or not she was aware of any link between not feeling well and Adrienne's behavior, she said that she hadn't made the connection at that point. She did admit that she had a nagging feeling that she needed to say something to Adrienne about her behavior.

One afternoon, as the group shopped for food at a local grocery store, Adrienne turned to Robin while in the checkout line and said, "Who was stupid enough to bag the lettuce this way?" knowing full well that Robin had been the one to do it. Robin said she felt "like someone punched me in the stomach" and instantly she made the connection. Deciding that her health was more important than keeping peace, she took Adrienne aside and told her the truth: "When you speak to me that way, I feel horrible. If you don't have anything positive to say, please don't speak to me at all!" Then she braced herself for Adrienne's response. To Robin's astonishment, Adrienne immediately apologized (common behavior for bullies who are confronted about their antics).

Robin did what most people do—she minimized Adrienne's behavior and ignored her own feelings to avoid the discomfort of conflict. It wasn't until her body stepped in with a physical alert that she paid attention. The body never lies. One of the best ways to identify where you need to stand up for yourself is by paying attention to your physical reactions. Your body will always help you identify when you need to speak up. As we saw earlier in chapter two, this is one of the primary ways that your feelings help you to take good care of yourself. For example, when someone violates one of your boundaries, you might suddenly feel tension in your neck and shoulders. Or when your friend calls to talk your ear off (and you let her), you may feel the hair on the back of your neck stand up as your anger rises with every passing word.

Too often we immediately numb our feelings rather than listen to their wisdom. For example, after a difficult phone call you might reach for high-carbohydrate foods to calm your nerves. Following another fight with your teenager you might plant yourself in front of the television to anesthetize your anger. One woman I worked with recognized that her fear of conflict was at the root of her inability to get a handle on her weight. After keeping a journal for two weeks about her eating habits, she noticed that whenever someone said or did something to push her buttons, she went straight to the refrigerator instead of addressing the issue.

WHAT ARE BOUNDARIES?

Do you have a hard time standing up for yourself? Do you keep agreeing to do things that you really don't want to do? Do you often feel guilty about putting your own needs first? It's time to set your boundaries!

If I were asked to name the one action step that would most develop emotional strength and improve your life, it would be "to create stronger boundaries." Based on my experience, weak boundaries are at the root of 80 percent of the problems I've observed among people who are struggling to live more authentic lives. When we allow others to step over our boundaries because we fear confrontation or the consequences of putting our own needs first, we end up feeling angry, frustrated, and resentful.

Now that you have a better sense of who you are and what you value, and you've begun to express your power more directly, it's time to start setting limits.

A strong boundary is like an energy field or "psychic barrier" that protects your body, mind, and spirit from harm. Imagine that this field radiates outward from your body, providing you with protection from any negative influences that could invade your personal space. For example, you might let your husband or wife stand close to you, but keep a stranger at more of a distance (a boundary that protects your body). Or you might allow a close friend to give you feedback about your work, but decide against hearing it from a stranger (a boundary that protects your mind and/or spirit).

Having good boundaries in place actually allows you to be more available to others in an intimate way. It also can prevent conflict. For example, instead of emotionally shutting down when you come in contact with a family member who puts you down, you use your emotional reaction as a signal that a boundary needs to be set. Once you inform your family member that it's no longer okay to treat you that way (and once you back up this boundary with action), you are then able show up at family events in a more relaxed and open-hearted way.

Take Action! Where Do You Need to Take a Stand?

The first step in learning how to stand up for yourself is to become more aware of when and where you need to set better boundaries. In other words, identify where you need more space, self-respect, energy, or personal power. Let's look at some examples of boundaries you might need to develop:

People may not . . .

Go through my personal belongings

Criticize me

Make comments about my weight

Take out their anger on me

Humiliate me in front of others

Tell off-color or racist jokes in my company

Invade my personal space

Gossip in my presence

I have a right to ask for . . .

Privacy

More information from a medical provider

A new hairstyle from an old stylist (or a new hairstylist)

Quiet while I'm trying to concentrate or relax

A rain check when I don't want to do something with a friend

Help around the house

More information before making a purchase

More time before making a decision

To protect my time and energy, it's okay to . . .

Turn off the ringer on the phone

Return calls or e-mails within a week (instead of a day)

Request that a friend or coworker be on time for our appointment

Bow out of a volunteer activity

Cancel a commitment when I'm not feeling well

Take an occasional mental health day

Reserve a place in my home that is off-limits to others

Delegate the tasks I no longer want to do

Now it's your turn. By completing the following three sentences, you'll get an idea of how you may need to set stronger boundaries. If you have trouble completing the sentences, it may help to recall a time when you felt angry, frustrated, violated, or resentful. Remember that your feelings are your inner guidance system and they will provide clues to ways in which you may have needed to stand up for yourself in the past.

Finish each sentence with at least 10 examples (or more). Don't censor your thoughts; just keep writing. Even the smallest examples are critical. Maybe you've been overcharged at the grocery store but blew it off by saying nothing. Or maybe on a night out with your girlfriends at a restaurant, you decide not to return your salmon even though it's overcooked because you don't want to make a "scene." Or instead of telling a friend who stops you on the way to your office that you don't have time to talk, you let her go on and on. These "little things" may seem inconsequential, but they are all great examples of how we give our power away, little by little, over time. You don't have to be weak to have these experiences. Some of the most confident clients I've worked with privately share examples just like these. As simplistic as it may sound, when you return a meal that's not cooked the way you want it, it's not just about that meal. It's about saying to yourself, and to the world, "I deserve to have what I want—and I respect myself enough to ask for it directly." Taking a stand has less to do with the specific situation you're facing and more to do with raising the level of your feeling of self-worth. Setting a boundary, although difficult, will increase your confidence and self-esteem. In turn, this makes it easier to stand up for yourself when faced with other situations in the future.

1. People may not . . .

_____

_____

_____

_____

_____

_____

_____

_____

2. I have a right to ask for . . .

_____

_____

_____

_____

_____

_____

_____

_____

_____

_____

3. To protect my time and energy, it's okay to . . .

_____

_____

_____

_____

_____

_____

_____

_____

Put this list aside for a week, and at the end of the week, pull out
the three lists and write down anything else that occurs to you.

Sometimes simply becoming aware of situations that require you to have stronger boundaries can be the key to creating them. Often I've found that people just need to give themselves permission to respect and honor their self-care. Although setting boundaries might appear selfish, it's actually an important way to respect the needs of others too. When you become aware of your boundaries (and begin to honor them), you naturally begin to consider (and respect) the boundaries of others as well.

Standing up for yourself by setting boundaries is one of the most powerful ways to build your self-esteem. Consider this analogy: Imagine yourself as a beautiful small building that has 10 floors, each one representing a greater level of confidence and self-regard. The top floor, the penthouse, symbolizes you at your best—self-assured, assertive, direct, and self-trusting. Every time you take a stand, set a boundary, or ask for what you want, you move closer to the penthouse—the place where you most want to live. On the other hand, each time you neglect to stand up for yourself, this same elevator moves down a floor or two. Do you want to live in the basement? I'm sure you don't!

Your actions move you either up or down. While it's inevitable that you'll make some mistakes, the more you practice standing up for yourself, the more you'll inhabit the fullness of who you are. There's good news: As you reach higher and higher levels of self-esteem, the downtimes will become smaller and smaller. Though you may sometimes find yourself doing something that diminishes your power, you'll recognize it quickly and rectify the situation. And as your self-esteem and confidence increase, you'll become unwilling to settle for anything less than what honors and respects who you are.

Anytime you stand up for yourself, you're in essence telling yourself and the world around you "I am no longer willing to give away my power." It's as if you make a deposit in your "spiritual bank account"—the account that allows you to withdraw the courage and confidence you need to stand up for your life!

There's another reason why standing up for yourself is important. You will undermine your success when you are unable to set boundaries. The reason is simple: Every time you neglect to take a stand or protect your time and energy, you send a message to yourself that you can't be trusted. Any kind of success, whether it's with your relationships, your finances, or your career, brings with it added responsibility and, as a result, an even greater need to set boundaries. If you don't stand up for yourself, you'll limit the opportunities you draw into your life, because you won't trust yourself enough to handle them. *If you cannot set and keep firm boundaries, you will always fear the added responsibility that comes with more success.*

Okay, enough convincing, let's get started.

Take Action! Prepare to Set Boundaries

Now that you've become aware of how you need to stand up for yourself, it's time to do something about it. Let's start by setting boundaries with others. There are five guidelines that I recommend when faced with having to have a difficult conversation. They are:

1. Set your intention
2. Get support
3. Discharge strong emotions

4. Tell the truth with grace and love

5. Debrief

As you choose the person that you need to stand up to, please know that the closer the person is to you (spouse or family member), the more challenging the conversation might be. We usually have the most loaded relationships with family members, especially when we have a long history of letting things go instead of dealing with them directly.

1. Set Your Intention

Before you set a boundary with someone, it's important to be clear about your intention. The highest intention when facing a difficult conversation with anyone in a healthy relationship is to move toward greater intimacy—to heal the relationship by telling the truth. As my friend Terrence Real, author of *How Can I Get Through to You?* says, "The way to a deeper, more intimate connection with others is to learn the dance of harmony, disharmony, and repair."

Telling the truth isn't easy. Especially when you've allowed the other person to behave in a way that undermines your self-esteem. Allowing the behavior means you've essentially condoned the behavior. Changing your mind will most likely come as a surprise to them.

Too often we communicate our needs indirectly using sarcasm or little jokes. My mother and I needed to face this issue in our relationship. As a young woman who was busy with her life, I didn't get home to visit as much as my mother would have liked. When I did, she often made comments like "Do you plan to stay longer than five minutes?" These comments hurt and ended up creating the opposite response of what she wanted—they made me want to stay away.

When I finally let her know how her comments made me feel, I was surprised and deeply touched by her response. She apologized and admitted that her own mother used to do the same thing. Embarrassed by the thought of passing on this legacy, we both agreed to stop being sarcastic with one another and start telling the truth about how we felt toward each other. To my mother's credit, she has honored this agreement till this day. As a result, our relationship couldn't be closer, and I can never get enough of seeing her.

While the intention is to repair the relationship, please remember this: No one, regardless of how close they are to you, has a right to steal your power. No one. I don't care if it's your mother, father, son, daughter, or close friend. There is never a reason why anyone should have your permission to put you down, disrespect you, steal your energy, or rob you of precious self-esteem.

Be clear about your intention. Are you confronting this person simply to vent your anger, get revenge, or repay them with your own criticisms? Or do you intend to let them know how they've hurt you and inform them of how you'd like things to change? Setting your intention is a powerful first step.

2. Get Support

When you're ready to start speaking up, asking for what you want directly, and stating your needs, you'll need the strong support of your partner or Life Makeover Group to back you up. Often support can mean the difference between success and failure. Facing conflict and standing up for yourself will require you to have difficult conversations, and one of the necessary components of being able to have those difficult conversations is having someone you can talk to both before and afterward. Having support in place is like having someone holding you up while you feel wobbly—and you will feel wobbly as you start to stand up for yourself. You'll make mistakes, you'll hurt somebody's feelings, and you will be ungracious in the way you speak to someone at first. That's all just a normal part of learning. You'll need to have loving people around you who can help you work through the inevitable mistakes you make and the unexpected reactions of others.

One of my former clients, Brian, found that having support paid big dividends. As the founding partner of a law firm, Brian knew that his business was poised for dramatic growth. All the signs for expansion possibilities were evident. He had a high referral rate from existing clients, he was considered a top expert in his field of tax law, and a national magazine was about to publish a feature story on his firm. In preparation for a high growth phase, I asked Brian to anticipate any obstacles that might get in the way of his success (an important question to address *before* the fact). He admitted that he had some reservations about his executive assistant.

His assistant had been with him for more than ten years, and he relied on her heavily to manage the office. Lately, important priorities were falling through the cracks, and she didn't seem as energetic and enthusiastic as she had been. Brian had brought this to her attention several times without seeing any change. But the thought of letting her go was unbearable for Brian. Like 85 percent of the business owners whom I've coached in the last fifteen years, Brian was willing to tolerate a less than competent employee, though it was hurting his business. He couldn't imagine having to fire her. Though Brian was a well-respected, confident, smart businessman, he would literally crumble each time I suggested that he needed to let his assistant go.

I asked Brian two important questions. First, "Do you honestly feel in your heart that letting your assistant go is the right decision?" Second, "If you had the support, plan, and language to let her go gracefully and with respect, would you do it?" When the answer was yes to both, we got to work.

Together, Brian and I came up with a plan for how I would support him through taking the critical step of finding a new assistant in order to expand his business. First, I asked Brain to create a profile of his ideal executive assistant. Next, he created a severance plan that he felt was fair and respectful of his current assistant's contribution. Finally, Brian developed the language he would use to tell her the truth with grace and love. We practiced this conversation until he felt comfortable and totally at ease.

Brian and I also discussed how he needed to avoid overexplaining why he was firing his assistant and simply return to the truth of the situation by saying something like "This is a difficult conversation for me to have with you. I have appreciated all that you've done for the firm over the years. Up until now, things have worked out well, but my needs have changed and I've decided to replace your position with someone more suited to the firm's current needs."

Although Brian's assistant was quite surprised and upset by his decision, she didn't scream or cry (the two things he feared the most). Instead they discussed a way for her to leave the firm with dignity. After Brian let his assistant go, he later admitted that without having the support to back him up, he would never have followed through with his plan, and it never would have gone as smoothly.

Remember that when you take those first steps toward standing up for your life, you may feel completely unglued, as if you might fall apart. After a difficult exchange or an unexpected reaction, having a partner to hold you up when you feel a little shaky will give you a chance to solidify your ability to stand up on your own. Give yourself the gift of knowing what it feels like to have that kind of support—you deserve it!

3. Discharge Your Emotions

The next critical step you'll need to take to prepare yourself to confront others is to vent how you feel with someone safe. Before you take a stand, you need to discharge any strong emotions that may prevent you from speaking in a neutral tone with grace and respect. To do this you'll need to discharge these emotions beforehand on your own or with a partner. If not, you run the risk of seriously damaging an important relationship.

My client Juanita had reached a boiling point with her eighteen-year-old daughter. For three nights in a row, her daughter, Maria, had ignored Juanita's curfew by coming home late. When Juanita and I talked, she was feeling horrible because of what had happened when Maria had come home the night before. Juanita had been furious and fed up with Maria's behavior. When Maria returned home at 2 a.m., Juanita was waiting to confront her. A fight ensued, and during the screaming match, Juanita got so angry that she threw her daughter out of the house.

If your intention is to heal your relationships, then it's important to remember this: *When there is defensiveness in any exchange, there cannot be any true communication.* Discharging your emotions beforehand allows you to move toward repair. If you do not have access to a support partner, you can vent your emotions by writing about how you feel in a letter that you never send or by venting your feelings out loud in a car or in front of your bathroom mirror. In addition, you might even engage in some form of cardiovascular exercise to blow off steam.

4. Tell the Truth with Grace and Love

The next step in setting boundaries is to develop and practice the language you'll use to speak the truth. By developing a script beforehand, and practicing it until it feels comfortable, you'll be better able to communicate your feelings and needs with respect and dignity for yourself and for the other person involved. Creating the appropriate language has three steps:

1. Acknowledge the importance of the relationship (when appropriate)
2. State your perspective starting with "I . . ."
3. Ask to have your needs met

To begin this process it's important to identify and clarify the truth. To do this, answer the following question:

> *If you could say anything without any negative consequences or ramifications, what would you say to this person?*

As you answer this question, don't try to be "nice." Just tell the truth directly without embellishing any details. Once you have a good idea of what the truth is, you'll be able to craft the language into a respectful and gracious script. Let's use some of the prior examples to demonstrate what I mean:

Example #1: People may not . . .

- Tell off-color or racist jokes in my company

The first step in telling Joan that you no longer want to receive any dirty jokes is to identify *your* truth—the truth you'll use to craft an appropriate response. For example, you might want to say something like "Joan, I can't stand it when you send me these ridiculous dirty joke e-mails. They annoy me and disgust me. Every time I get one from you, I just want to call you up and scream. I should have done it a long time ago!" While getting to your truth, lay it on the line without worrying about how appropriate it sounds. Once you know the truth, you're ready to craft your response to, in this case, Joan, with grace and love.

When developing the language, use your partner for support. For example, your group might help you come up with a way to say something like this to your friend:

> *"Joan, I wanted to be honest with you about something that's been bothering me, so that it doesn't get in the way of our relationship. I have a policy of not accepting off-color jokes by e-mail. I realize that you were unaware of this, so I'd just like to ask you to take my e-mail address off of your list. Thanks so much."*

By saying it in this way, you are taking responsibility for the fact that by accepting her behavior up until this point, you've essentially told Joan that it's okay.

Let's look at more examples:

- Take out their anger on me

Once you've discharged your emotion by identifying your truth, you might say:

> *"Carol, it's not okay to yell at me. If you're willing to lower your voice, I'm willing to discuss this with you. Otherwise I'll need to leave until you calm down."*

- Humiliate me in front of others

> *"Jim (the boss), I know you were upset about the inaccuracy in my report, and I apologize for the mistake. In the future I'd like to discuss problems like this in private instead of in front of others."*

This last example always makes people uncomfortable. I usually hear things like: "You don't understand, I can't afford to risk my job" or "If I said that to my boss he'd fire me on the spot." While I understand that you may put your job at risk by telling your boss the truth, there are two other important things to consider: 1) If you can't *afford* to stand up for yourself, you need to improve your financial health; and 2) The cost of compromising your integrity and self-esteem is far greater than any job. Often a boss is unaware of how damaging his or her behavior is to an employee. You might be surprised at how quickly he or she makes a change for the better with a little feedback.

Example #2: I have a right to ask for . . .

These types of boundaries are related to your needs. By asking for what you need you give others a chance to care for you and serve you well. This makes for healthier relationships all around. When making these requests, keep it simple and be direct. Here are some examples of what you might say:

- A new hairstyle from an old stylist

  "Jonathan, I love what you've done with my hair, and I'm ready for a change. I'd like to talk about a new hairstyle."

- Time to myself

  "Mike and Sally, Mom needs time to herself. You'll need to play in your rooms for the next half hour while I read. Please do not disturb me."

Once you set this boundary, DON'T let them disturb you—be firm! With children, it will take consistency on your part before they'll learn to respect your boundaries. Don't give up!

- More information from a medical provider

  "Doctor Samuels, before we finish our appointment, I'd like more information about your diagnosis. Tell me more about additional testing, how many cases of this you've treated, and where I might find more helpful data about this illness."

If you receive shocking news, always reserve the right to come back with your questions within a short period of time. For example, you might say "Will you please tell the nurse to schedule some time for me early next week?" If the answer is no, find another physician!

Example #3: To protect my time and energy, it's okay to . . .

- Return calls or e-mails within a week (instead of a day)
- Turn off the ringer on the phone
- Bow out of a volunteer activity

Experience has taught me that most of us just need permission to do or not do the kinds of things that will give us more time, space, and energy. As you set limits that protect your time and energy you'll need to determine the best guidelines for your particular situation. For example, your job may not allow you to return calls within one week, but you may be able to extend the response time by a day. Or you might decide to turn off the ringer on your phone at 8 p.m. every evening while a friend may choose 5 p.m. on weekdays. You need to decide which boundaries work best for you and your family.

When bowing out of a volunteer commitment, try something like this:

> *"Tom, I know I agreed to head up our fundraising efforts, but after reviewing my schedule, I now realize that I won't be able to give it my best attention. I'll need to bow out. I'd like to help you find a replacement by the end of next week."*

Setting boundaries will probably feel uncomfortable at first. But like any new skill, it will get easier over time. Remember, when setting boundaries you cannot control another's response or behavior; you can only deliver the message with grace and love. Stay true to yourself and, in the long run, everyone wins.

There are a few more things to remember about setting boundaries. You don't need to overexplain, defend, or debate your position. Your needs are always valid. If you're not able to give your time and attention to a volunteer activity, you deserve to take care of yourself. If you're not able to baby-sit for your sister's kids this weekend because you haven't had a weekend off in six months, you just need to honor your need for time off. Don't make up excuses. Honor your integrity by telling the truth.

Start with easy boundaries first and, as you get stronger, tackle the more challenging ones. Always back up your boundaries with action. If you relax your boundaries by giving in, you essentially invite people to ignore your needs. For example, when you tell Joan not to send you any off-color jokes, she may very well forget. You'll simply need to remind her. As a matter of fact, I often suggest that clients include this reminder in their original conversation. So if we continue with Joan as an example, you might say something like:

"Joan, I wanted to be honest with you about something that's been bothering me, so that it doesn't get in the way of our relationship. I have a policy of not accepting off-color jokes by e-mail. I realize that you were unaware of this, so I'd just like to ask you to take my e-mail address off of your list. I know there's a chance you might forget, but don't worry. I'll be

sure to gently remind you when it happens again. Thanks so much."

Other examples of language you can use in common situations are:

"Grace, I've noticed lately that when I receive your phone messages, I hesitate in calling you back. I realized that I feel drained of energy when you complain about how your husband doesn't treat you right. I haven't been honest with you, and that's not fair to our relationship. I want you to know that I will support you one hundred percent in doing something to heal your marriage. If you'd like me to help you find counseling or a book that might be useful, I'll be right there to support you. But I can no longer listen to you talk about issues with your husband."

By the way, in considering the example above, it's important to note that when you allow a friend or family member to dump their anxiety or frustration on you, it not only affects your emotional and physical well-being, it buys them more time to avoid dealing with the problem. Unfortunately some of us need to feel a whole lot of pain before we take action to remedy a difficult situation. Don't rob loved ones of an opportunity to do something about a problem by temporarily taking on their pain.

"Julia, I have a policy of not accepting personal calls during work hours. I'd love to talk with you; can we schedule a call tomorrow evening?"

5. Debrief

When you decide to set a difficult boundary or have a conversation that makes you feel shaky, it's important to have support in place for *after* the conversation as well as before. For example, if you need to tell your father that you can no longer work for his company, you'll want someone in place to debrief with who will validate your choice and help you get back on solid ground. It can be just the reassurance you need to proceed with a difficult conversation, knowing that a safe, loving person will be on the other side to greet you.

Take Action! Setting Your Internal Boundary

There is one more boundary I'd like to tell you about. In her book *Facing Codependence,* Pia Mellody introduces the idea of having an "internal boundary"—a psychic shield that protects you from internalizing the responses or reactions of others. While you can set clear boundaries with those who treat you poorly, the truth is that there will always be critical, judgmental people in your life. Rather than take their comments or feedback personally, using an internal boundary will allow you to decide what you're going to let in and what you're going to reject.

An internal boundary is like a filter we put over ourselves as a way to determine how we'll process the judgments, comments, criticisms, or feedback of others. For example, when going in for your annual review at work, you'll want to have your internal boundary firmly in place, so you can decide three things: first, which feedback feels accurate; second, which feedback feels inaccurate; and third, which feedback needs further consideration. Having a strong internal boundary in place means that you are well insulated from any inappropriate comments from others. It does not mean that you're cutting yourself off from your feelings; it means that you are protecting them.

It's important to distinguish an internal boundary from putting up a wall. When you put up a wall you essentially cut yourself off from the person who's speaking to you as well as from what they're saying. When you use an internal boundary, you are connected and interested in what the other person has to say, but you're protected from what isn't true. In that way, an internal boundary allows you to be connected and protected.

The next time you are about to have a conversation that makes you feel a bit edgy, or have an interaction with someone who normally pushes your buttons, imagine your heart protected by a beautiful glass shield. Place your hand over your heart and call upon the voice of your inner ally for support. For example, you might say something to yourself like "I know I have what it takes to have this conversation with grace and love. I am a strong man with a good heart. I will remain calm and open to hearing what she has to say and, if necessary, I will ask for more time to consider her thoughts."

Use this shield as your internal boundary and you'll not only care for your soul, you'll keep your power to yourself.

Finally, in order to stop giving your power away to others, be aware that you *will* end up disappointing or hurting someone along the way. That's just a fact of life. For example, if your mother expects to hear from you every single day and you decide that you just can't do that anymore, her feelings might be hurt when you tell her the truth. By saying something like, *"Mom, my schedule no longer allows me to talk to you every day. I'm busy at work and I need time to myself when I get home. I know this change is going to feel uncomfortable for a while, so maybe we can make the transition by talking once or twice a week instead,"* you are setting a boundary that respects your mother's feelings. That's all you're responsible for—telling the *truth* with grace and love.

Now it's your turn . . .

Take Action! Set a Boundary

The person I need to set a boundary with is:

_____

My intention is:

_____

My support person will be:

_____

To vent my emotions I will:

_____

The raw truth is:

_____

I will tell the truth with grace and love by saying:

_____

I will have this conversation by (date/time):

_____

As you continue with this program, remember the following:

- Each time you neglect to ask for what you need, or to confront someone who treats you poorly, you chip away at your confidence and self-esteem.

- The body never lies; it will always help you to identify when you need to speak up.

- Good boundaries allow you to be more available to others.

- If you cannot set and keep firm boundaries, you will always fear the added responsibility that comes with more success.

RESOURCES

Books

How Can I Get Through to You? by Terrence Real (Scribner, 2002)
Real offers the tools every therapist and client needs to achieve a radical new vision of love.

Facing Codependence: What It Is, Where It Comes From, How It Sabotages Our Lives by Pia Mellody (Harper, 1989)
Mellody is a pioneer and authority on codependence. This book provides a clear understanding of how people who are raised in dysfunctional environments are set up to put the needs of others before their own.

CHAPTER FIVE

Build Your Courage Muscles

W HEN I WAS A YOUNG WOMAN I was painfully shy. I wore little makeup, dressed in a fairly nondescript way, and went out of my way to avoid drawing attention to myself. The word "courage" was not in my vocabulary. In my late twenties all that changed with an invitation to an event that would unexpectedly shift the direction of my life.

My friend Suzanne invited me to a Toastmaster meeting (an international speech club) to watch her give a presentation. I sat quietly in the back of the room and listened to her, as well as to other members of the club, deliver their speeches. At the end of the meeting, I was invited back. Impressed by the courage of the group and the supportive nature of the way they gave feedback to each other, I accepted their invitation.

Several meetings later, the leader, Dick Skinner, asked me to consider giving a five-minute "icebreaker" speech introducing myself to the group on my next visit. I immediately panicked. I was happy to sit back and watch, but the idea of getting up in front of the group more than terrified me. At the same time something inside me felt challenged by his request. There was a tiny bit of excitement at the thought of doing something so daring. So, I agreed to give the speech.

Over the next week I thought about the icebreaker. Each time I considered giving the speech, my hands would start to sweat, my heart would beat faster, and my throat went dry. I couldn't imagine getting up in front of a group of people to tell them about myself. During the week, when I shared my fear with Suzanne, she encouraged me to take one small step and put together a few notes about what I *might* say if in fact I did decide to do the icebreaker. I spent the next day writing about my personal and professional life. Eight pages later I had more than enough to say.

As the day to deliver my speech drew near, I became increasingly anxious. I called Suzanne and told her that I had decided not to go and asked her to please thank the members of the group for their invitation. Suzanne wouldn't let me off the hook. If I couldn't bring myself to give the talk, she asked me to at least show up at the meeting, reminding me that the policy of the group was to not pressure anyone into speaking. Rather than simply "chicken out," she suggested that I attend and tell the group the truth: I wasn't ready.

The appeal to my integrity worked, and I reluctantly agreed. On the morning of the meeting day, however, I woke with laryngitis. But with the grace of God (and my notes hidden neatly in my pocketbook), I went anyway.

When the meeting began, Dick asked if I was ready to give my speech. I explained that I had laryngitis and was too nervous to speak. Honoring the policy of the group, Dick accepted my decision and moved on. While others began to give their speeches I felt a sadness wash over me. Deep inside a little voice challenged me to change my mind. One by one, with each speech I listened to, this little voice became stronger and, as the end of the meeting drew near, Dick asked one more time if I wanted to give it a try. Without thinking I said yes, laryngitis and all.

The walk to the podium was one of the longest I'd ever taken in my short life. All the way there I listened as my inner critic berated my decision: "How could you agree to do this? What are you thinking? Look at all these people staring at *you*! You're about to make a complete fool out of yourself!"

When I arrived at the podium I realized that I had left my notes in my pocketbook. Too uncomfortable to go back, I opened my mouth to speak. Nothing came out. My voice was gone. I tried again, and one by one, each person in the audience began to smile and nod their heads in my direction. I loosened up a little and started again. This time I was able to squeak out a few words, and before I knew it I was off and running. To this day I can still remember my lips sticking to my teeth. I couldn't for the life of me tell you what I said, but I can tell you what I felt when I sat back down and listened to the feedback from my evaluator: sheer joy.

My evaluator, Helen Chen (I still remember her name), gave me positive feedback about my speech, and believe me, I know she was stretching. She said things like "You're a natural" or "You make great eye contact" and "You have a soothing voice." I sat in my chair, knees shaking, heart pounding, taking it all in. When I left the meeting that day something inside me had changed. I felt more confident, less self-conscious, and I was suddenly able to look strangers in the eye. It was my first experience feeling the power that comes from building my courage muscles by overcoming fear.

When I look back over my life, that Toastmaster meeting was the beginning of my freedom. The love, support, and positive feedback from the members opened a door inside of me—a door to the life that I have now. Locked behind my fear was a hidden gift, one that led me to my calling. I often think about how my life would be different had I not had faced that fear. Since that first meeting many years ago, I've faced some of my greatest fears. Fears like the death of a loved one, the painful ending of significant relationships, and a health crisis. Throughout it all, one of the greatest gifts has been the strengthening of my faith and my courage muscles—gifts that have served me well.

How is your life limited by your fear? What are you not doing that you'd really like to do? When we use fear to our advantage by tackling those things that evoke a sense of excitement and trepidation, fear becomes an ally. Each experience provides a challenge and an opportunity to expand your comfort zone. The way to create an extraordinary life is to make the challenge of fear work for you by building your courage muscles.

USE FEAR TO YOUR ADVANTAGE

In this chapter I'd like to challenge you to begin using your fear as a tool to build courage. You've already begun to build your courage muscles. The decision to make your personal development a top priority by letting your power shine through and by standing up for yourself is a courageous act. Now it's time to consciously use your fear to build even more courage and self-trust. By building these muscles you'll retrain yourself to become someone who naturally wants to face fear instead of someone who wants to avoid it.

Before we start, let me tell you what this chapter *isn't* about. When I talk about building your courage muscles, I'm not suggesting that you take up bungee jumping or parachute out of a plane. While these types of activities take an enormous amount of courage, and would build your courage muscles, I want you to think even bigger. I'm talking about saying yes to your life! I want you to take those steps (large or small) that will keep you moving closer to the person you are meant to be. I want you to train yourself to face fear head-on, so you can push yourself beyond a mediocre life to a life that honors your values and highest calling.

How will your fear serve you? It will keep you on your toes and warn you of potential danger. Fear will help you to focus and offer you a way to recognize right from wrong. Fear can challenge you, motivate you, and energize you to act. For example, have you ever given a presentation at work or taken a test and felt so much energy and strength afterward that you were ready to tackle something else? When you make friends with fear and step outside of your comfort zone, this zone expands. Then things that used to frighten you or seemed impossible become easier.

Facing fear builds confidence and emotional strength—the strength that allows you to make a difference in the world. The more you work with fear, the more your confidence grows. Too often we hold ourselves back from taking important steps that will improve the quality of our lives, hoping that our fear will go away. For example, you might hold off on making a career change because you're afraid that you won't make as much money or be as successful doing something you love. Instead you continue in your present job as if one morning you'll wake up and miraculously have the courage to try something new. If you wait for your fear to dissipate or disappear, trust me, you'll have a long wait. Anything worth doing in life will involve fear—whether it's talking to a stranger, giving a speech, or leaving a relationship that you know is holding you back.

Take Action! Identify Your Fears

Let's take a look at some of the things you fear that might be holding you back from doing what you want to do. Take out your journal and list six things that immediately come to mind:

1. I'm afraid _____
2. I'm afraid _____
3. I'm afraid _____
4. I'm afraid _____
5. I'm afraid _____
6. I'm afraid _____

WHAT DOES AVOIDING FEAR COST YOU?

Avoiding fear robs you of the rich experiences that make life meaningful. For example, there are so many people afraid to fly who dream of seeing Europe or taking their kids to Disneyland yet never will. While you might be afraid to risk rejection by asking someone to dinner, or face loneliness when you decide to move across the country to a place you've always dreamed of living, the costs of not acting are far greater. Over time, as we give in to fears such as these, our world gets smaller and smaller.

Before you know it, years have flown by and you're left with a whole lot of regrets. As a matter of fact, I've seen the direct correlation between a life held back by fear and the dread of approaching birthdays or other milestone dates like New Year's Eve. *When you're not saying yes to life in spite of your fear, you will always dread the passing of time.*

In addition to missing out on all that life has to offer, fear drains your energy and power. When you hold yourself back from taking an action that you know you should take, this "holding out" can take more energy than it would to face your fear and act. For example, if you have a physical symptom that frightens you and you put off going to the doctor, every day you wait drains you of energy whether you realize it or not. If you're in a marriage that feels dead, the longer you avoid addressing the issue, the more you lose power. When you allow your power and energy to be depleted, you are less likely to act, because there is, literally, less of you available.

Take Action! Let Fear Be Your Teacher

How would your life change if you used your fear as an ally? What are the benefits of facing your fear? The first step in building your courage muscles is to get leverage. Take out your journal and answer the following questions:

- *What changes would you make in your life if you had no fear? What would you do? Where would you go? Who would you want with you?*

_____

_____

_____

_____

- *Imagine that you're at the end of your life; what would you most regret not having done?*

_____

_____

_____

_____

- *How will you (and your life) benefit from stronger courage muscles?*

_____

_____

_____

_____

- *What else might you be able to do if you faced some of these fears?*

_____

_____

_____

_____

- *Are there any items on your list that make you feel a mix of excitement and fear?*

_____

_____

_____

_____

I have a special litmus test for whether or not to act in spite of fear. If, when my clients consider a situation, they feel a mixture of fear and excitement, I've learned that a "yes" vote is usually a good bet. There seems to be something about this combination that signals an opportunity that will move the client forward in his or her life.

On the other hand, sometimes fear can teach you about yourself by revealing your limitations. I learned this lesson well from a woman named Katherine. Katherine decided to participate in a quantam leap exercise with a team of friends. Participants were expected to climb to the top of a 25-foot pole, stand on a small disk and eventually jump off trusting teammates to guide them to safety. As part of the team Katherine had attempted to climb the pole, but when she neared the top, she felt paralyzed by fear and was unable to stand on the disk. She came back down feeling discouraged and relieved. At the end of the exercise, when everyone else had made it to the top, Katherine decided to try again. She felt anxious to be part of the success of the team. When she reached the top of the pole this time, once again Katherine felt terrified by her fear, but after some coaching from her teammates below, she was able to stand up.

At the end of the program, as we debriefed, Katherine felt angry with herself for going up the pole the second time. The terror she felt at the top was overwhelming, and she realized that she should have listened to her inner voice that told her to stay on the ground. In this situation Katherine realized that her fear was actually trying to warn her to take better care of herself.

There are other benefits to facing your fear. Often facing one fear opens a doorway to unexpected success in other areas of your life. My client Cameron learned this lesson in a powerful way when he saw how his fear of flying was linked to his stalled career.

When Cameron was in his early twenties, he took his first commercial flight, with two brothers to the Caribbean where they were vacationing together for a week. On the flight home the plane hit a severe storm, and the pilots, unable to navigate around it, asked the passengers to brace themselves for some heavy turbulence. The plane bounced around, and at one point dropped a good 500 feet in the air. Cameron was terrified and thought for sure he was going to die.

The flight was such a frightening experience that for several years Cameron wouldn't go near a plane. At the time we began our work together I was unaware of this event. Cameron had decided to work with a coach to help him move forward in his career.

Cameron worked in sales for a high-tech company. He loved his job but wanted to earn more money and eventually work his way into a more senior position. When I asked him what might be preventing him from making this transition, he responded by saying: "I just don't know. Every time my sales seem to take off, something gets in the way."

Over the next three months Cameron worked on increasing his sales performance and gaining greater exposure within the company. True to form, each time Cameron was about to shift to a new level, something blocked his path. For example, the morning that Cameron was scheduled to make an important presentation to his boss, his car broke down and he arrived two hours late for work. Then, after laboring six months on landing a big new account, the potential client received some bad press, causing their stock price to tumble. As a result they made a decision to hold off on doing the deal.

One day Cameron came to the coaching call anxious to talk about a dream he had had the night before. In his dream he was taking off in an airplane to go to a sales conference, where he was expected to deliver a speech about overcoming objections. When his plane took off it got caught up in high-tension wires. Hanging in midair, Cameron immediately woke up.

Cameron's excitement to share the dream came from a vague inner knowing that there was some kind of link between his fear of flying and his career success. Trusting his inner guidance system to lead him in the right direction, I referred Cameron to a professional who specialized in treating fears and phobias with a new, fast-acting technique called the "Emotional Freedom" technique. After two sessions with the counselor Cameron uncovered the link.

The symbolism of flying and taking off was indeed directly related to his fear of success. He discovered that on a subconscious level he feared the travel requirements that might come with a management position in sales. Cameron realized that if he were going to choose sales as a career path (something he loved), he would most likely have to get on an airplane at some point or another. Cameron needed to face his fear of flying in order to unlock the connection between the two.

After his sessions with the phobia specialist and studying a good book on overcoming his fear of flying, Cameron was ready to get on a plane again. Fortunately his first flight was fine. By facing his fear with support and preparation, Cameron developed enormous courage, which served his career well. One year later, after a lot of hard work and dedication, Cameron was promoted to sales director.

Whether you're afraid to fly or to sign up for a word processing class makes no difference. What feels scary to one person may feel like a piece of cake to another. The only way to learn how to face the challenge of fear is to practice, practice, and practice. Let's get started!

Take Action! Build Your Courage Muscles

To begin the process of building your courage muscles you'll want to set yourself up to succeed. Any courageous act can be made easier with the right inspiration and preparation. To do this you'll need three things:

1. Support
2. A history of success
3. A courage talisman

As you've already learned, having someone in place both before and after taking a difficult step is a necessary requirement for success. That way, regardless of the outcome, you end up with a loving friend who makes you feel great. There are a number of ways to use the support of others. For example, if your leap involves giving a speech, you might ask a few friends to listen as you practice your delivery. If you need to make amends to someone you've hurt, have a friend available to speak with you once you've had the conversation. Or if you feel nervous about your first trip abroad, speak to someone who's been there so you know what you're in for.

The next way to set yourself up to succeed is to create a personal reminder of your strength and ability to handle what comes your way. To do this, take out your journal and write the following:

Three challenges that I've successfully handled in the past are:

1. _____

2. _____

3. _____

When I asked my client Morgan to do this exercise she picked the following three situations:

My divorce

Going back to school to finish my degree

Facing an empty nest

Next, I asked her the following three questions:

1. What qualities of character allowed you to handle these challenges?

2. In what ways were you resourceful?

3. What did you learn from these experiences that might serve you now?

Here's what she said in response to the questions:

In each of these situations I called upon my patience and ability to persevere in times of great stress. I have a strong mind and a sense of determination. When I decide I'm going to do something I can count on myself to do it. I'm smart enough to reach out to my friends when I'm upset about something, rather than lashing out and hurting someone. This helped me immensely with my divorce and when my two children moved out on their own. Finally, after raising my children, I've become more resourceful and organized. When I set goals, like completing school, I'm able to break down my plans into manageable steps and find the help I need to methodically get the work done. I've learned that I can accomplish anything with a plan, good friends, and a strong belief in myself.

By doing this exercise Morgan was able to create a written reminder of her strengths and abilities. By flagging this page in her journal she was able to refer back to it during those times when she felt afraid and questioned her ability.

Now refer back to your three challenges above and answer the following questions in your journal:

1. What qualities of character allowed you to handle these challenges?

2. In what ways were you resourceful?

3. What did you learn from these experiences that might serve you now?

Mark these pages in your journal so you can refer back to them easily for support when needed.

Finally, as you prepare to build your courage muscles, I'd like you to find some symbol of courage—a talisman of sorts. My friend Nathan uses a small statue of the lion from *The Wizard of Oz*. My friend Michelle uses a special phrase—"zero fear"—when she needs to be reminded of her strength and courage. One year, when I made a conscious decision to build my courage muscles, I hung the following quote by Georgia O'Keeffe on my office wall to remind me of my commitment to act in spite of my fear:

I've been terrified every day of my life but that's never stopped me from doing everything I wanted to do.

What will you use as your mental security blanket?

Remember, when you take well-prepared action in spite of your fear, you gain energy. The excitement that comes from pursuing something that will change your life for the better will fuel your efforts. Now it's time to take action!

Take Action! Play the "Face Your Fear" Game

As you begin to face your fear, think of this process as a game. The object of the game is to build your courage muscles. The prize is the courage, confidence, and emotional strength to live your life to its fullest. Here are the rules:

- You must choose one assignment from each of the seven categories below.

- Your courage partner or Life Makeover Group must review your choices to make sure they are challenging enough. If you are playing the game alone, be sure and push yourself beyond your comfort zone!

- You must complete all seven assignments within thirty days (if you choose a long-term assignment, such as moving, you must start the process within the 30-day period).

There are seven categories to choose from. Read through the examples and choose one assignment from each category. If the examples do not apply to you, create your own assignment and add it to the list in the appropriate place.

Once you've chosen seven assignments, you'll then need to review them with your partner or Life Makeover Group. To make sure that you're choosing items that will challenge you to stretch outside of your comfort zone, ask your partner or support team to raise the stakes (based on what they know about you) by making an item more challenging or by adding something completely new to your list. For example, if you decide to be bold and share your poetry with friends, your partner or group may challenge you to share your poetry at an open mike night instead.

Remember that there is no judgment. One person's assignment might seem easier than another's. For example, if you have an outgoing personality, walking into a room full of strangers and introducing yourself might seem easy. But to a shy person this action may represent a very large step. The idea is to choose assignments that challenge you to move outside of *your* comfort zone.

"Face Your Fear" Game

Here are the seven categories:

1. Fulfill a secret dream
2. Stand out from the crowd
3. Tell the truth
4. Be bold
5. Face a physical fear
6. Face a professional fear
7. Face a financial fear

1. Fulfill a Secret Dream

For years I harbored a secret dream to dance. I loved watching performers like Michael Jackson spin their magic on the stage. While listening to music in my car I often choreographed dance moves in my head. I kept this dream to myself, deciding that I was too old to ever dance professionally. But when I was thirty-one years old I learned about a "street funk" exercise class that gave me a chance to fulfill my secret dream

The class was taught by an amazing young man named Carleton Jones, a dancer who had performed on Broadway and with Janet Jackson and Paula Abdul. My first visit to the class reinforced the voice of my fear that said I was too old to dance. The class was one and a half hours long, and it was hard. During one of the classes Carleton announced that the Dance Company was putting together their annual performance in Boston and he would be choreographing the street funk performances. Carleton encouraged anybody who was interested in performing in this production to sign up and study with him for three months. When he made this announcement I felt excitement wash over me; then I was flooded with fear. Because I had created a habit of responding to these feelings with action, I agreed to participate in the performance at once.

In the beginning I felt anxious on my way to every single class. After rehearsing for a month I started to settle down and enjoy the pleasure of fulfilling this important dream. When I look back at the night of the performance I still smile when I think about how excited I was to dance with such a wonderful group of people.

Now it's your turn. What do you dream about doing? Here are some possible assignments:

_____ Plan a trip to a place you've always wanted to visit

_____ Audition for a part in a local play

_____ Run for public office

_____ Participate in a fantasy sports camp

_____ Write a book

_____ Learn to fly or sail

_____ Learn to paint, sculpt, or draw

_____ Exhibit at an art show

_____ Design your own website

_____ Sing in front of others (for example, you might find a Karaoke night)

_____ Your assignment: _____

2. Stand Out from the Crowd

What's the one thing you could do to stand out from the crowd? Too many of us have been taught to blend—to fit in with others' expectations and desires. If you want to be a leader in your life, you'll need to get comfortable standing on your own. My client Jennifer was surprised when I suggested that she learn to stand out from the crowd with a simple first step—wear a new color nail polish: metallic blue. Always the conservative one of her friends, if Jennifer wore nail polish at all, it was pale pink or clear. Although it sounded like a strange request, it was actually a safe and fun way to practice doing something out of the ordinary that felt a little risky.

What will you do to stand out from the crowd? Choose from one of the following assignments:

_____ Change your hairstyle

_____ Have dinner by yourself

_____ Wear something out of the ordinary

_____ Sing a solo in your church choir

_____ Write a letter to the editor of your favorite newspaper

_____ Dress one step up from others at work

_____ Share a strong opinion or different point of view

_____ Speak up at a town meeting

_____ Be the first one on the dance floor

_____ Wear a stylish hat

_____ Your assignment here: _____

3. Tell the Truth

George earned a tremendous amount of courage by telling the truth. In his mid-twenties George had a serious gambling problem. While working for a bank, he secretly stole money to support this habit. After six months he had embezzled several thousand dollars. Years later, when he was in recovery for his gambling addiction, George decided to tell the truth as part of making amends for his past. He made an appointment with the bank manager, explained his past behavior, and offered to arrange a way to pay back all of the money. The bank manager was stunned by his admission of truth and, after several conversations with other bank officials, explained to George that not only had the stolen money been written off, the statute of limitations had passed. They would not be pressing any charges. While George was relieved and empowered by telling the truth, he knew he wasn't finished. He decided to make regular donations to a local charity until he had contributed the exact amount of money he had taken from the bank.

As you learned in chapter three, sometimes telling the truth means standing up for yourself. This can be a very powerful way to build your courage muscles. Is there someone you need to be honest with? If so, feel free to include this person as an assignment below. Otherwise, choose one of these:

_____ Set a limit with a family member

_____ Apologize for hurting someone's feelings

_____ Ask someone to stop sending you junk e-mail

_____ Admit to a past mistake

_____ Tell someone about your overspending

_____ Let someone know that they've hurt your feelings

_____ Ask someone to stop talking too much

_____ Tell a coworker, friend, or family member that you are no longer willing to participate in gossip

_____ Admit to and deal with a problem in a relationship

_____ Correct any false information on your resume

_____ Your assignment here: _____

4. Be Bold

Early in her career Hannah worked as an executive assistant to a business owner in her hometown. As his assistant she managed his office as well as his personal affairs. The first Christmas that they worked together Hannah received a substantial holiday bonus in the form of a check. The second year, however, she received a small gift—a basket of candy. Hannah had worked even harder during her second year and had counted on receiving another monetary bonus. When she and I spoke she said she was shocked and insulted by the gift.

I explained that in order to honor her self-esteem and maintain her self-respect, Hannah needed to be bold and tell her boss how she felt. Rather than sit with the anger over the holidays, I encouraged her to pick up the phone and call him right away. She agreed, and with knees shaking she told her boss exactly how she felt. To her boss's credit, ten minutes later he was at her door with an apology and a check.

What bold action will you take?

_____ Place (or respond to) a personal ad

_____ Compliment a stranger

_____ Sign up for an improvisational acting class

_____ Give a speech

_____ Speak up when you receive bad service or when what you get is not what you ordered

_____ Enter a debating contest

_____ Change a holiday ritual with your family

_____ Ask someone out on a date

_____ Campaign and speak up for an unpopular cause you're passionate about

_____ Negotiate the price of a purchase

_____ Your assignment here: _____

5. Face a Physical Fear

Learning a new sport or physical activity can be a great way to expand your comfort zone. When my client Jonathan finally learned to Rollerblade he was surprised at how easy it was. For three years Jonathan had put off learning this new sport out of a fear of looking awkward and falling. When he mentioned this desire to his support team one of the members offered to give him a lesson. Together he and this friend went to a large parking lot and spent the afternoon helping him learn how to brake and turn corners.

Jonathan was surprised at how quickly he picked up the sport. Afterward, not only did he feel like a million bucks, he was thrilled to be invited on a trip to rollerblade in Central Park with a singles group he had recently joined. Jonathan had the time of his life!

Is there a physical challenge you're ready to take?

____ Learn to ski

____ Make a dentist's appointment

____ Get help to overcome a phobia (snakes, spiders, or fear of heights)

____ Make a geographic move

____ Learn to mountain bike, swim, or Rollerblade

____ Parachute out of a plane

____ Make a doctor's appointment

____ Quit smoking

____ Get on a scale

____ Schedule corrective surgery that you keep putting off

____ Your assignment here: _____

6. Face a Professional Fear

For three years Andrea, a massage therapist, had talked about raising her fees. Compared to her colleagues, Andrea's work was seriously undervalued, and yet she was too afraid to risk losing her existing clients. But the cost of inflation had made it difficult for her to make ends meet, and she finally had to face her fear head on. I suggested that Andrea conduct some research to determine the going rates for massage services. When she reported her findings I challenged her to increase her fees over and above the highest price she had uncovered in her research. Andrea took the challenge and created a letter to send to her clients. Not only did Andrea keep all of her clients, with her courage muscles strengthened she was pleasantly surprised by her new ability to suddenly face other fears that had been tormenting her for years.

How will you expand your professional comfort zone?

____ Make 50 cold calls

____ Start a new business

____ Ask for a raise

____ Ask for referrals

____ Hire someone

____ Fire someone

____ Purchase a computer or a new piece of equipment

____ Raise your fees

____ Refer out any non-ideal clients

____ Put a career change in motion

____ Your assignment here: _____

7. Face a Financial Fear

William finally got up enough courage to face the fact that he was seriously in debt. For months he had been spending money on everything from new clothes to gifts for his friends. When the damage was assessed William was shocked to find that he was more than thirty-five thousand dollars in debt. He contacted a credit-counseling agency and put a new debt elimination plan in place. Although William learned that it would take him quite a long time to pay back the money, he felt relieved and determined to stay on a smart financial path.

What financial fear will you face?

____ Get a copy of your credit report

____ Meet with a debt consolidation company

____ Open your bills-to-be-paid folder

____ Get your taxes done

____ Repay an old debt

____ Ask for money owed to you

____ Balance your checkbook

____ Tally your debts

____ Cut up your credit cards

____ Make and stick to a budget

____ Your assignment here: _____

Go back and review each category and list the assignments you've chosen here:

1. *I will fulfill the following secret dream* _____

2. *To stand out from the crowd I will* _____

3. *I will tell the truth by* _____

4. *I will take a bold step by* _____

5. *To face a physical fear I will* _____

6. *To face a professional fear I will* _____

7. *To face a financial fear I will* _____

Now you're ready to get to work! Be sure to use your support team. As you embark on building your courage muscles, I'd like to share some advice from my on-line community to make your process easier:

Take action quickly. Don't let your anxiety build over time. For example, if you decide to make a long overdue doctor's appointment get in as soon as you can, even if it means putting yourself on a cancellation list.

Celebrate your mistakes. Remember that it's okay to make mistakes. In fact, making mistakes is mandatory when learning to build your courage muscles. See any mistake as a sign to ask for help or move in a different direction.

Change your mind. If you decide to take an action that suddenly doesn't feel right, trust yourself. Know your limitations and give yourself permission to change your mind.

When in doubt, check it out. If you feel like your physical or emotional well-being may be at risk, check it out with someone you trust. Ask someone you feel is more courageous than you are for help.

Give yourself a deadline. Don't confuse planning with acting. To really move forward in your life you'll need to set a "by when" date and stick to it!

Be accountable. Ask your partner or team to hold you accountable for your commitments. Being challenged by others can provide instant inspiration and motivation.

Let's put it together:

My support person will be_____

The five past successes I will call upon for courage are:

1. _____

2. _____

3. _____

4. _____

5. _____

*My courage talisman will be*_____

Ready, set, go! Play the "Face Your Fear" game so you can say yes to your life! From now on, when you feel afraid, get excited! See it as an amazing opportunity to build the kind of courage muscles that will allow you to make your greatest contribution to the world!

RESOURCES

Books

Courage: The Heart and Spirit of Every Woman: Reclaiming the Forgotten Virtue by Sandra Ford Walston (Broadway Books, 2001)
This book shows women, their daughters, friends, and the men who support them how to reclaim their forgotten birthright and live more fully from their hearts and spirits.

Women of Courage: Inspiring Stories From the Women Who Lived Them by Katherine Martin (New World Library, 1999)
Forty women describe life-altering moments in which they had to rely on their own inner resources to conquer challenges and find strength and wisdom.

Still I Rise by Maya Angelou (Random House, 2001)
Maya Angelou celebrates the courage of the human spirit over the

harshest of obstacles. This poem is a tribute to the power that resides in us all to overcome the most difficult circumstances.

Maiden Voyage by Tania Aebi (Ballantine Books, 1989)
A story of one woman's courageous journey around the world in a sailboat. A true tale of courage.

Websites/Organizations

www.toastmasters.org
Toastmasters is an international speech club that supports members in learning the art of public speaking. Everyone has an opportunity to practice conducting meetings, giving speeches, and offering constructive evaluation.

www.emofree.com

This is an amazing website that offers resources on a simple and effective treatment for fears, phobias, and a wide range of physical symptoms including anxiety, depression, and body pain.

CHAPTER SIX

Pass Up Good for Great

THERE ARE TWO GREAT ASSETS that we all have temporary ownership of in our lifetimes: time and energy. In order to live a life that honors your personal and spiritual development, and your commitment to make the world better in some way, you must direct these assets toward those things that are aligned with your values. To do this you must be able to exercise the patience and maturity to pass up good for great.

We are each given the gift of free will. With this gift comes a responsibility to make wise choices. By becoming highly selective about how you will and will not use your time and energy, you acquire a more mature perspective on life. You realize that less is often more, and that quality is far better than quantity. You also recognize that because your outer life is a direct reflection of your inner life you must develop patience and a sense of mindfulness about what you will and will not let into your life.

When I talk about passing up good for "great," I'm not talking about feeding an insatiable hunger for material possessions. A hunger for more "things" is born from spiritual deprivation, a longing for something deeper and more nutritious than any car or house can ever offer. I'm talking about a quality of greatness that is directly in line with your spiritual standards. The standards that create the right emotional and physical environment you need to be your best self. Wanting better is not selfish or self-indulgent, it's the by-product of high self-esteem and a deep understanding that we are all entitled to a high quality of life. There is nothing immoral or selfish about having high standards. As a matter of fact, *as you learn to pass up good for great, it will fuel your desire and your ability to support others in doing the same.* Deprivation breeds fear and selfishness, the opposite of a generous spirit. Abundance breeds love, generosity, and a deep desire to serve our fellow human beings.

Developing the ability to pass up good for great is a natural next step in your spiritual growth. As your sense of self-worth deepens, you recognize that you deserve more from life and you allow yourself to have it. You stop settling for less. Of course there is risk involved in using this skill—the pain of disappointment, the fear of loss, or the feeling of being an outsider when you choose a different path than others close to you do. It is this fear that keeps many of us from having high expectations. Instead we learn to settle for, and hang on to, what is safe and familiar or what is expected of us. A typical example of this is the man or woman who settles for an unsatisfying relationship out of a fear of being alone or not being able to find someone better. Or the person who stays at a secure job in spite of the void he or she feels inside from not expressing their true talents or gifts. As the old saying goes: "The devil you know is better than the devil you don't know." Fortunately, I don't buy that.

SPIRITUAL STANDARDS

Now that you're well on your way to standing up for your life, there's one last skill to develop: the ability to honor a set of spiritual standards that will support you in becoming very choosy about what you allow into your life.

Spiritual standards are the rules or guidelines you put in place to honor your spirit—the essence of who you are. They are your gold standard. By using them as a guide you ensure a greater quality of life. When these standards are respected, you bring your highest self to each life experience. You protect your time and energy by becoming more selective. This may feel a bit uncomfortable as you learn to want more for yourself than you've wanted before. This is why most of us get in our own way when it comes to accepting great things into our lives. We settle for less, fill up our time and space with too much "stuff," and cling to what's mediocre out of a fear of losing what we have. When we finally get up enough courage to hold out for something better we're usually well rewarded for our effort.

In order to pass up good for great you'll need to develop the patience and emotional strength to *sit with wanting something that's good* (like a new job) *while you pursue something that's great* (the right job that utilizes your best talents and skills). This will be challenging at first. We live in a society that reinforces a need for instant gratification. Fortunately, the more you use patience, the more patience you'll have, and the easier it will be to hold on until that which is in your highest interest appears.

Learning to pass up good for great also means that you'll have a chance to strengthen your faith in a power greater than yourself. There will be plenty of times when it's necessary to pass on good without knowing what great will be. While this will be difficult at first, it provides you with an important opportunity to surrender your willfulness and witness the amazing gift that having faith in a Divine presence has to offer.

As I've learned to honor my standards by passing up good for great a Divine force has opened unimaginable doors to accelerate the progress of my personal and professional growth. I've seen this same principle operate in the lives of my clients too. In order to help her honor her spiritual standards, my client Anna decided to surround herself with people who were also engaged in their inner work. To do this she was challenged to end a "good" relationship to make space for one that was more aligned with her standards for a great relationship—one that was deeply fulfilling. Although it was difficult, once she made peace with her decision and mustered the courage to let it go, a new, healthier relationship appeared at just the right time. As you make the choice to honor your spiritual standards by passing up good for great, a Divine presence often delivers more than you could ever imagine.

While we each have our own unique set of spiritual standards, I've come to see a pattern of standards that are shared by those clients who successfully lead their lives. These universal standards are:

1. I center my life around my values.

2. I strive to live a life of integrity where my thoughts, words, and actions are aligned with my spiritual self.

3. I surround myself with people who are committed to their own inner work.

4. I engage in work that reflects my values and inspires me to be my best.

5. I make my emotional, physical, and spiritual well-being a top priority.

6. I respect others and resist the temptation to judge them based on my standards or beliefs.

7. I am committed to living a life that serves a greater purpose.

Take Action! Define Your Spiritual Standards

As you consider these spiritual standards, choose the ones that you might want to incorporate into your life. Then add your own to the list. Put your new spiritual standards here and/or in your journal:

1. _____	6. _____
2. _____	7. _____
3. _____	8. _____
4. _____	9. _____
5. _____	10. _____

In order to honor these new standards you'll need to start practicing the skill of passing up good for great. As you do, get ready for your life to change. Let me share an example of what I mean.

THE "IDEAL" CLIENT

Years ago, when I first began my coaching practice, I agreed to work with anyone who wanted to hire me. Like most business owners, I was anxious to gain experience and I wanted to build a secure source of income. As time went on it became clear that there were certain types of clients who inspired my best work and allowed me to better honor my values. As a result of this discovery I created an exercise called the "ideal client profile." This profile allowed me to easily identify those clients who would command my best work.

Not only did I begin using this exercise in my own practice, I shared it with clients who were ready to raise their standards too. It had dramatic results. I remember one woman in particular, Pauline, the owner of a small accounting firm. Pauline was tired of her business and was seriously considering selling her practice and moving on to something else. When I asked her to define "tired" she said she no longer felt challenged by her work and was fed up with handling the details of business, like collecting money from clients who didn't pay on time. Rather than rush into something as serious as selling her business, I introduced Pauline to the concept of passing up good for great and suggested that she set a new standard for her work.

Pauline was settling for less by working with demanding clients who drove her crazy. She was bored with a majority of her work and, having paid her dues, it was time to respect her spiritual standard of honoring her emotional, physical, and spiritual health. To do this I asked Pauline to reflect back over the last several years of her professional experience and make a list of those clients who were the most inspiring, fun, and rewarding to work with. Once she completed this list I then asked her to transfer the top 10 clients to a new list.

Next, I had Pauline identify the common characteristics that each of these ten clients shared. For example, were they mostly male or female? Was there a specific age range? Did they work in a particular industry, share similar needs or personality traits? As she identified these common denominators she began to see patterns that helped her with the next step. I then asked Pauline to review her list and choose the seven characteristics that she felt were most important. These formed the profile of an exceptional client, one who inspired her best work. Her list looked like this:

My great clients:

1. Own their own businesses

2. Have a high level of integrity

3. Appreciate my work

4. Pay on time and can easily afford my fees

5. Have a sense of humor and are fun to be with

6. Have more complex accounting issues and/or a strong plan for growth

7. Treat me like a partner and respect my input

Once she had this profile in place I asked Pauline to answer a few questions. How did she feel about the idea of only working with these types of clients? If she could, would she still feel called to sell her practice (a perfectly fine decision)? Would she be willing to move toward working exclusively with ideal clients to see how that made her feel?

Pauline agreed to give it a try, so I had her print out three copies of her new ideal client profile and put them in clear view—by the phone, in her appointment book, and on her computer's screensaver. By keeping this profile in view she would internalize the characteristics quickly and, holding this image in mind, she would actually begin to draw these types of clients toward her.

Now that Pauline had identified "great" by knowing exactly the kind of person she most wanted to work with, she needed to use this profile to choose wisely when considering new clients. I warned her that she would most likely be tested. There was a good chance that she would receive calls from people who *almost* fit the profile—but not quite. Her challenge would be to pass up good for great. Potential clients needed to be ideal in order to make the cut.

In the beginning Pauline made the mistake of accepting a couple of less than ideal clients. This was a normal part of the learning curve and only served to remind her of what she no longer wanted in her business. Over time she had a firsthand experience of the kind of Divine power that really did have her best interest at heart. As she stayed true to her list, ideal clients started showing up—almost exclusively.

Eight months later Pauline was amazed at how her business had changed. She had a thriving practice filled with terrific clients who appreciated and valued her service. Her business was earning more money than ever before, and she looked forward to going into the office every day. The choice to honor her standards by passing up good for great not only dramatically improved the quality of her life, it improved the quality of her service. In that way, her clients benefited from her decision too!

Take Action! Define Your Ideal

The "ideal profile" exercise can be used in a variety of ways to honor your spiritual standards. For example, when my client Rick said he was interested in making new friends who shared his commitment to his spiritual development, I had him profile an "ideal buddy." This profile included the qualities, interests, and spiritual beliefs that were most aligned with his own. Or when my client Nicky was about to hire a new administrative assistant, I had her create an ideal profile by considering the type of assistant that would support her in doing her best work. It's much easier to pass up good for great when you've clearly defined what "great" means to you.

Now it's your turn. Choose an area of your life where you need to set an ideal in order to pass up good for great. For example, if you'd like to meet a romantic partner, you might need to profile an ideal mate. Or if you've decided to look for a new job, you might want to profile an ideal company. You can even use this exercise when making a purchase or a major decision. For example, you might profile your ideal new home or an ideal new school for your child.

Set your ideal in place now. Fill in the blanks below.

I need to create an ideal profile for _____

My best case scenario is _____

My top seven characteristics are.

1. _____
2. _____
3. _____
4. _____
5. _____
6. _____
7. _____

Once you've defined your idea of great, it's important to honor your criteria. Challenge yourself not to settle for anything less than what you really want. For example, if you're an employer looking to hire an ideal candidate, be patient while you interview as many people as it takes to find the best. If you're a business owner who has clearly defined your ideal project, be willing to walk away from a good project in order to keep the space open for a great one. Trust me, it will be well worth the wait!

Let's look at another way to pass up good for great: by using the *Absolute Yes* test.

THE "ABSOLUTE YES!" TEST

In *Take Time for Your Life*, I offered readers a simple, yet powerful way to honor their top priorities: by creating an *"Absolute Yes* list." This list consisted of seven items that readers deemed most worthy of their time and energy. The *Absolute Yes* list became the governing document that allowed readers to make wise choices. If it wasn't on the list, it wasn't a top priority.

I took the concept of an *"Absolute Yes"* a step further by using it as a way to test whether or not something was important enough to get my time and attention. It has become an important tool that helps me and my clients make decisions that honor our spiritual standards. For example, my client Laura used the *Absolute Yes* test as a way to honor her spiritual standard of making her self-care a top priority. For example, whenever she was invited to a social gathering, she'd ask herself the following question before she responded: "Is this an Absolute Yes?" If the answer was anything but a resounding "yes!" she said no.

My friend Sophia used the *Absolute Yes* test in a different way. One of her values was beauty, and Sophia had a spiritual standard of honoring this value in all aspects of her life. Whenever she shopped for clothing or home accessories she checked in to see if her purchase was an *Absolute Yes* before making a decision. That way, Sophia was able to maintain high standards about what she allowed into her closets and into her home.

I have learned to trust this test by allowing it to guide the choices I make in all areas of my life, from which restaurant I choose to which business opportunity I should or shouldn't pursue. It's never let me down. It takes courage and practice to use this test when making decisions. In the beginning there will be plenty of times when you're tempted to say yes to something that's a "maybe" or a "not bad." Once again, you need to stand firm in your commitment to pass up good for great. If it's not an *Absolute Yes,* the answer is easy—it's a no.

Take Action! Use the Absolute Yes Test

Stop for a moment and consider any major decisions you're currently faced with right now. Is there a purchase you need to make? Do you need to choose a new direction for your work? List three decisions here:

1. _____

2. _____

3. _____

Then ask yourself the following question: "Is this an *Absolute Yes?*" You'll know the answer almost as soon as you ask the question. An *Absolute Yes* usually feels like a solid, immediate

"Go for it!" Get in the habit of using this question with simple decisions too. For example, when choosing a movie or vacation spot. Trust your feelings to lead you down the right path. You may not know what's coming, but if you keep your standards high, I can pretty much guarantee you that it's something great!

CHOOSE WISELY

As you continue with the process of standing up for your life, make the idea of passing up good for great your guiding principle. Use this principle in all areas of your life. For example, I pay close attention to what I allow into my mind. This means that I am always filtering my choices about what I'll read, watch, or listen to through the lens of "Will this honor my highest good?" As an example, one night while watching television I turned to a prime-time show about a murder in New York City. At the moment I hit the channel I was pulled into an intense, provocative scene. I immediately became engaged in the drama. Two minutes into the story I realized that while this show might be highly entertaining, it only represented "good." The violence and suspense were not the best choice for my sensitive nature. As soon as I became aware of my choice I decided to pass up good for great by turning the channel to something more emotionally uplifting.

My client Amanda used this principle to help her make wise choices about her relationships. Amanda was in her late twenties and had a busy social life. She went out almost every night and had a variety of friends that she spent time with. In spite of the number of people she had in her life, Amanda said she felt lonely and disconnected.

As we looked at her relationships, Amanda admitted that many of her friends were really just acquaintances with whom she enjoyed a pleasant if superficial connection. They'd hang out or meet for drinks and their conversations always revolved around gossip or their latest dating escapades. Amanda wanted more.

As she became more invested in improving the quality of her life, she longed for deeper connections that went below the superficial level of conversation to something more emotionally and spiritually rewarding. Addressing the delicate issue of her relationships, Amanda carefully assessed the quality of each one. She had to limit her time and energy to those people who shared her desire for a more meaningful connection. This meant letting go of some relationships, investing more intentionally in others, and proactively seeking new friends who shared her interests.

You can learn to use your time and energy in a way that honors your gold standards by making wise choices in little ways every day. For example, you might:

- Allow yourself to spend extra time with a friend instead of rushing off to another appointment.
- Pay the small delivery fee to have your groceries and other goods delivered rather than going to the store.
- Spend time with your family after dinner rather than rushing to clean up.
- Treat yourself to the theater rather than spending another night in front of the television.

By practicing this skill in little ways each day you'll find that it has a cumulative effect. Over time you'll not only realize that even small choices can have a significant impact on the quality of your life, but you'll raise the bar on your expectations and with it the level of your self-worth.

Take Action! Create a Daily Habit of Passing up Good for Great

Challenge yourself throughout the day to use your new skill of passing up good for great. You might even use the following question to guide your choices:

If this is good, what would be great?

Reinforce this new habit by taking a few moments at the end of each day to record your success in your journal. Not only will this strengthen your ability to pass up good for great, it will provide you with the motivation you need to make even better choices continually.

As you continue to make wise choices that honor your spiritual standards you'll learn to trust that a power greater than you always has your best interest at heart. Ask your support team or partner to hold you to your spiritual standards. At those moments when you are most tempted to settle for less, take a deep breath and wait. In your waiting you will find the inner strength and maturity to accept what you truly deserve—nothing less than great.

RESOURCES

Books

A Year to Live by Stephen Levine (Bell Tower, 1997)
A beautiful guide to making choices that really matter by living this year as if it were your last.

Dancing at the Edge of Life by Gale Warner (Hyperion, 1998)
This is a deeply moving account of a young woman's last thirteen months of her life. An award-winning poet and journalist, Gale captured her extraordinary journey of coming face-to-face with death and life, in these powerful and poignant journal entries. While this book may be hard to find, it's worth the search.

Living a Life That Matters by Harold S. Kushner (Knopf, 2001)
One of my favorite authors, Kushner writes about the importance of making a difference in the world by affecting the life of even one person in a positive way. In doing so, we prove that we do in fact matter.

CHAPTER SEVEN

Center Your Life
Around Your Values

W HEN OUR LIFE BECOMES A TRUE EXPRESSION of our values we make our greatest contributions to the world. We feel inspired, eager to start the day, and at peace with ourselves knowing that we are fulfilling our greatest potential. The reward that comes from doing the inner work outlined in this book is the courage and confidence to live a life of meaning and purpose—a life that honors your values.

By now you should feel more empowered. You should feel centered and grounded in who you are. Your confidence and self-esteem should be stronger and more abundant. You've now integrated the necessary skills to express yourself with power and grace. Congratulations! Now it's time to bring this work out into the world.

As I mentioned in chapter one, our purpose in life is twofold. First, we need to make a conscious commitment to our personal and spiritual development, elevating our thoughts, words, and actions to a higher, more enlightened level. Second, we must move beyond our selfishness and contribute to others so that we leave this world a significantly better place than when we came here. Now that you've focused your energy on your

195

inner work, it's time to orient your outer life around your values so that you can set the stage for how you will contribute your talents and gifts to others.

In this chapter there are three areas that we'll focus on. They are:

1. Values
2. Life changes
3. Action

To begin centering your life around your values you'll need to reconsider the work you did in chapter two to see how your values might have changed as a result of your work thus far. Next you'll have a chance to reevaluate the three life changes you chose to make once you're clear about your essential values. Finally, with those two pieces in place, I'll show you a simple three-step process to implement these changes so you can start to center your life around your values. Let's get started.

Take Action! Revisit Your Values

As you strengthen your inner skills by changing the way you behave in the world, it's important to reconsider your values. Over time your values may shift in reaction to how you evolve and as circumstances change in your life. To begin the process of orienting your life around your values, take a fresh look at your four essential values on page 68 and copy them here:

Four Essential Values from Chapter Two:

1. _____

2. _____

3. _____

4. _____

Now that you've done that, go back and retake the values test in chapter two so we can see how your values might have changed as a result of the work you've done so far. Once you're finished with the test, list your four essential values here (whether they've changed or not):

Values Now:

1. _____

2. _____

3. _____

4. _____

Now that you're clear about your four essential values, the next step is to revisit the three life changes you chose to make in chapter two on page 76 after completing your first values exercise. To begin this process, list the earlier life changes here:

Life Changes from Chapter Two:

1. _____

2. _____

3. _____

As you look over these changes, how do you feel? Are they still the changes you need to make in order to orient your life around your values? If so, do they feel as daunting as they did in the beginning? If they no longer feel appropriate, how do they need to change? If you decide to make the changes more challenging or to alter them in any way, I'd also like to recommend that you take a moment to acknowledge how your personal development throughout the last several chapters might have affected this desire. How have you grown? What qualities of character have you strengthened?

When it came time for my client Rachel to reevaluate her values and the life changes she thought she needed to make in order to honor these values, she was surprised to find that while her values had stayed the same, all of her life changes needed to be modified. Rachel said she no longer felt like the same person, and the changes she originally chose to make—change her job, end a significant relationship, and go back to school—were all attempts to fill a void in her life. Now the time and energy she was spending developing a new relationship with herself had filled this void.

Rachel's realization is a common one. Too often we attempt to make major life changes in reaction to something else that isn't working in our lives. When we do this we either set ourselves up to fail or choose a direction that ends up being temporary or ultimately unfulfilling. When you build a solid relationship with yourself you make smart life choices. Choices that come from a deeper, more centered place, a place that brings true fulfillment.

Now feeling stronger, confident, and more able to stand up for herself, Rachel realized that she needed to do things a bit differently. She made a decision to stay in her relationship and continue the work started in chapter four, by asking to have her needs met and by keeping her boundaries firmly in place around the time she needed to herself. Rachel also decided to stay at her current job in order to improve her finances. She realized that her energy was being drained by her debt and that handling that problem was a higher priority than changing jobs. Finally, Rachel also put going back to school on hold while she worked hard to get her finances in order. She realized that finishing school for the sake of getting a degree without a smart career plan might well be a foolish move. She needed to research and explore her career options before making such a large investment of time and money.

When Rachel finished reevaluating her life changes they looked like this:

1. Improve my relationship with Kevin.

2. Eliminate my debt.

3. Explore new career options.

My client Paul decided to take a different path. As a result of making a deeper commitment to the needs of his soul he decided to step out on a limb and risk in a big way. Paul was single, in his late thirties, and ready to pursue a lifelong dream. When he revisited his values and life changes he found that they were still exactly the right choices. A district attorney turned criminal defense lawyer, Paul had a hidden desire to be a comedian. His values were:

1. Educate others   3. To have fun

2. Laughter   4. To catalyze

Paul was smart and naturally funny, and for a long time he had kept his dream of being a comedian hidden. After all, who would be crazy enough to give up a lucrative career in law for a tentative try at comedy. By clarifying his values and developing enough trust in himself, he realized that it was time to do what he loved: Educate people about themselves using humor. Paul decided to make his career a top priority. His life changes looked like this:

1. Make a transition out of the legal profession.
2. Pursue career as a professional comic.
3. Move to Los Angeles.

Paul knew that he was taking a risk. Many of his friends and family members thought he was nuts. But Paul persisted, believing in himself and his dream. His action plan looked like this:

1. Create a financial plan to support my new endeavor.
2. Investigate the life stories of successful comedians.
3. Develop my material.
4. Perform at a local open mike night.
5. Research Los Angeles living options.

Take Action! Revise Your Life Changes

Now it's your turn to consider the life changes you need to make. Review your original life changes that you carried forward on page 197, make any necessary revisions, and list your three life changes here:

Life Changes Now:

1. _____
2. _____
3. _____

Remember to consider all aspects of your life: your home, relationships, emotional, physical, and spiritual well-being, etc.

Now that you know your values and the life changes you'll need to make to honor these values, it's time to get into action. Here's an effective and productive way to make these changes, using a simple three-step process:

1. Brainstorm your way to a plan of action
2. Anticipate and handle any obstacles
3. Act

These three steps are the basic philosophy that I follow whenever I start a new project or set out to make any kind of major change.

Take Action! Brainstorm Your Way to a Plan

You may already know the specific actions you need to take to begin implementing your life changes. If so, list ten action ideas in your journal (as you read on about the power of brainstorming, you may feel inspired to make a few changes!). If not, one of the best ways to overcome blocks and determine your first steps is to call upon the wisdom of others. In his 1937 book *Think and Grow Rich,* Napoleon Hill suggested that readers create a "Master Mind" group of individuals to support them in achieving their goals. Back then Hill understood the value of community, and his book was my first introduction to the power of group mind. I immediately set out to create my own Master Mind group and found it to be enormously helpful. This experience led me to use brainstorming formally as a fun and easy way to find any solution to a problem, or to identify any creative idea necessary to move forward with a plan. For the last 15 years I've relied on this step to kick start my favorite projects.

Because orienting your life around your values can feel risky, it's easy to feel blocked creatively or paralyzed by fear. A brainstorming session with friends or coworkers (strangers too!) will give you new ideas, great resources, and plenty of energy to get started. When you gather people together for the sole purpose of generating great ideas, amazing energy gets released and miracles start to happen.

I recommend conducting your brainstorming session in one of two ways. You can invite a large group of people together to brainstorm just for you, or you can make it a smaller group (six to eight) and let everyone benefit. There are advantages to both. When I've needed quick ideas, such as the names of people who can provide certain services, I've invited ten to fifteen people to join me on a conference call. I always offer to be of support in return. I've used smaller groups when I've wanted to hold ongoing meetings as part of a community of like-minded friends. Years ago I belonged to a brainstorming group that met at a local bookstore café once a month. That group was the catalyst for many of my successes, including my dream of becoming a published author.

To set up this type of brainstorming session you need to:

- Invite a group of energetic and positive people to your home or office. Tell them you'll be brainstorming for an hour or two and invite them to bring a need of their own. If you're working with a partner, each of you should invite two people to join you so that you have a total of six.

- Keep it positive (no yeah, buts!).

- Eliminate discussion or debate.

- Write down all the ideas.

- Keep an open mind; you never know when one silly idea may lead to a fantastic breakthrough!

Make the brainstorming session a festive and productive occasion. For example, you might hold a potluck dinner or serve appetizers and dessert. Make sure everyone benefits. Ask each participant to bring a specific need they would like to brainstorm and be sure to use a timer. It's important that everyone gets a chance, and there's nothing more off-putting than someone who takes up all the time.

When considering potential participants think beyond family and friends to acquaintances, colleagues, or people from your professional network. You might even consider some of the people with whom you do business such as your massage therapist, dental hygienist, lawyer, or accountant. I've found that some of the people you'd least expect to be interested, are interested, when given an opportunity to join a group of people who are excited about achieving their goals. You'd also be pleasantly surprised by the level of interest people have in sharing ideas and supporting the success of others.

To make setting up your first brainstorming session easier I've designed an e-mail invitation that you can send to potential participants. Modify this invitation to fit your needs:

Dear Friends,
I've recently decided to_____ (change careers, move to a different part of the country, find a new school for my son, etc.). To

help me move forward with this goal in a productive and effi-
cient way, I'm hosting a brainstorming session in my home on
the evening of _____. As someone who has demonstrated a
commitment to success, I thought you might be interested in
participating by bringing a goal or need of your own. This is a
great opportunity to get some creative ideas and resources that
might help you to move forward quickly and easily. If you're in-
terested in joining us, please send a reply and I'll get you all the
details. Thanks!

Each time I've conducted a brainstorming session the level of
creativity that gets expressed when people come together to
help one another always amazes me. Let's look at an example of
what I mean.

I met Debbie during a weekend workshop I was giving at
Mile Hi Church in Lakewood, Colorado. Debbie loved to ski.
In her early fifties, she recently had recovered from an illness
that had kept her bedridden for six months and she was now
ready to make some life changes. While discussing the benefits
of brainstorming I asked for a volunteer to demonstrate the
power of group mind. Debbie raised her hand immediately.

Debbie said she wanted to be a fulltime professional ski instructor. She loved to ski and wanted to share this love with others, but she was concerned about her age and her physical
ability after her illness. When she shared this with the other
members of the workshop she got a long list of ideas within a
few short minutes. Here are ten examples of what she received:

1. Offer a class for people who would love to ski but are
   afraid. Post a "skiing for chickens" flyer advertising this
   class in your church bulletin.

2. Call ski schools to see when they're hiring.

3. Develop a class for more mature skiers.

4. Contact five ski instructors and conduct informational interviews.

5. Read biographies of people who started new careers after age sixty for inspiration.

6. Visit the National Ski Association website for more info.

7. Develop your own special training strategy to build confidence and a unique reputation.

8. Do something to bring back the feeling of how it felt to learn how to ski.

9. Invest in your physical health. Start a new weight-training program.

10. Research some of the physical concerns that older clients might have.

Debbie was surprised and energized by the response of the group. As she listened to the great ideas, her hesitation and fear diminished. By the end of the workshop, Debbie was raring to go.

In the same workshop, Victoria raised her hand to go next. She said that she wanted to combine her language skills with her love of travel to earn a living. She also mentioned that she loved food. Immediately the group went to town coming up with possible action steps. They included:

1. Become a traveling interpreter.

2. Research jobs as a tour guide.

3. Consider working for an international company that offers relocation services for its employees.

4. Consider a position as a restaurant reviewer for a travel magazine.

5. Research culinary schools in Europe.

6. Start your own research company for people who want to live overseas and who need information on schools, job opportunities, or housing options.

7. Become a travel writer reporting on restaurants from around the world.

8. Become a courier for an international courier company.

9. Teach English part time in a foreign country.

10. Visit the library with a goal of uncovering 50 potential jobs that combine travel and languages.

Like Debbie, Victoria was excited about all the creative ideas generated by the group. That's what happens when you brainstorm with others. The best of humanity shines through. The natural desire to give, as well as the excitement of realizing that anything is possible, inspire people to show up for one another. As people feed off of each other's ideas, the energy of the group creates more. Not only does the person who is receiving the support get a whole lot of possibilities, they tap into the energy and enthusiasm of others and strengthen their belief that anything is possible.

Now it's your turn. Once you've completed your brainstorming session, list ten action ideas here:

1. _____   6. _____

2. _____   7. _____

3. _____   8. _____

4. _____   9. _____

5. _____   10. _____

Take Action! Create Your Action Plan

Once you have a list of ten ideas or more from your brainstorming session, review them and choose five action steps. If you feel nervous about moving forward, it's perfectly okay to choose easy steps. If you want a strong start, choose the steps that are more challenging (these are probably the ones that you'd rather not do). Whenever you embark on making specific life changes it's important to always put a simple action plan in place. This means choosing five items to get you started and putting them *in writing* to keep you on track. Make sure they are specific and doable. As you consider which five to choose, remember the litmus test: Look for those actions that make you feel a sense of excitement and nervousness when you consider taking them.

When Victoria looked over her list of ideas, she chose the following five actions to get her started:

1. Contact two international companies to see if they ever use traveling interpreters.

2. Research jobs as a tour guide.

3. Visit the library and research jobs that combine language and travel.

4. Pick up several travel and food magazines for ideas and to see what kinds of articles combine travel and food, as well as to learn more about the writers.

5. Contact two writers by e-mail to set up informational interviews.

What are your five actions? List them here. This list is the foundation of your action plan.

1. _____

2. _____

3. _____

4. _____

5. _____

Now you're ready for the next step:

Take Action! Anticipate and Handle Any Obstacles

Before you start taking action you'll need to plan for success. This means that you'll need to anticipate and handle any potential obstacles that might get in your way or prevent you from moving forward *before* they happen. As you look over your actions, ask yourself the following questions:

• *What might get in my way?*

_____

_____

- *What am I afraid of?*

_____

_____

- *What do I need to do to set myself up for success?*

_____

_____

As you consider these questions write the answers in your journal. Then determine the actions you need to take to set yourself up to succeed and add them to the top of your action list.

Let's look at an example. Let's imagine that you'd like to redecorate your home to make it a more soul-nurturing environment. You have your action list in place and you're ready to go. When you consider your actions you realize that two of the obstacles you face are a lack of time and fear that you may not have the necessary talent. So, to set yourself up to succeed, you add the following actions to the top of your list:

1. Give up one night of television or socializing and use this time exclusively for this project

2. Purchase a good book on interior design to see if I have the necessary skills to take on this project

When I asked Victoria to consider the potential obstacles that might prevent her from moving forward, she replied: "I'm concerned about my husband. I don't know if he'll agree to the idea of me traveling for work. Also, I'll need to have good child care in place for my teenage daughters." This is important information. It's easy to see how these two potential obstacles would prevent Victoria from ever making the important changes that would honor her values. The support from our closest loved ones is key to our success. In order for Victoria to believe that she could actually consider this change she'd need to add the following two action steps to the top of her list and put two original action steps on hold:

1. Set up a meeting with my husband to discuss my goals and child care issues.

2. Talk to my mom about her availability and desire to help out with the girls.

By tackling these two actions first Victoria would be increasing her chances of continuing with this process. Otherwise, I can guarantee you that she'd begin to sabotage her success. Too often we neglect to handle the pressing needs that most concern us when we think about moving forward with aligning our lives with our values. By considering her potential obstacles and building them into her action plan, she not only gave herself an edge, she increased her motivation and excitement. Victoria's new action plan looked like this:

1. Set up a meeting with my husband to discuss my goals and child care issues.

2. Talk to my mom about her availability and desire to help out with the girls.

3. Visit library and research jobs that combine language and travel.

4. Read through several travel and food magazines for

ideas, and to research articles that might combine them both.

5. Contact two writers by e-mail for informational interviews to explore the idea of freelance writing while traveling.

When I asked Debbie to consider her potential obstacles she said that her biggest concern was whether or not she was physically up to the challenge. While she had recovered from her illness fully, she was still feeling a little vulnerable emotionally. To address this issue I asked Debbie what she needed to do to prove to herself that she could handle the position. Debbie said that she needed to improve her physical conditioning and she needed some kind of reminder that she could do this.

To address these obstacles I suggested that Debbie add the following two action steps to the top of her list:

1. Meet with a personal trainer to discuss my health and get a program to build up my strength.

2. Ask three friends to check in with me weekly for the first month to remind me that I have what it takes to fulfill this goal.

Five months later I received an excited e-mail from Debbie saying that she had finally gotten up the nerve to apply to two major ski lodges in Colorado and she received offers from both! Debbie is now a full-fledged professional ski instructor.

Take Action! Uncover Your Real Obstacle

It's important to determine a real obstacle versus a perceived obstacle. Often we get caught up in familiar language and neglect to identify the real concern. For example, my client May said she wanted to be a pastry chef and that her obstacle was a fear of failure. This is a typical response. Upon hearing this I assured her that in fact failure *would* be a part of her experience. To demonstrate this I asked May if she had ever made something that didn't come out right. "Yes," she replied, "plenty of times."

"What did you do when that happened?" I asked. "I just tried it again until I got it right." "Okay," I said, "so you know how to handle failure. What's really going on then? What are you really concerned about?"

May said that her real fear was that people wouldn't like what she baked. Once again, probing further, I asked if she had ever baked for her family or friends. "Yes," she replied, "they all love my baking." "Well," I said, tongue in cheek, "are they from another planet? Are they somehow different than other normal people?" May laughed and, getting the idea, looked deeper for the true obstacle.

Underneath May's generalized fear was a legitimate, specific concern that she lacked the necessary knowledge to be a pastry chef. As she talked about this fear her eyes filled with tears—a good indication that we'd gotten to the root of her potential obstacles. Facing this truth was an important first step for May. Now she had something to work with. She simply needed more information. May decided to add "research pastry chef schools and classes" to her action plan. Interestingly enough, the very next day May found a flyer for a French baking class offered in her community. Seeing this as a Divine sign, she immediately signed up.

What are you *really* concerned about? Go back and look at

how you answered the questions about your potential obstacles on pages 208–209. Then take out your journal and answer the following questions:

- Are these obstacles the true obstacles or just a cover for something else?
- Is there something lying beneath these concerns?
- What's really going on?
- Rewrite your real obstacles here:

1. _____

2. _____

3. _____

4. _____

5. _____

_____

FLEX YOUR NEW COURAGE MUSCLES

There are a variety of potential obstacles that may prevent people from taking the necessary steps to orient their lives around their values. Fear is on top of the list. Since you've already begun to build your courage muscles, this should be less of a problem. It's easy to think that the fear we feel when starting out will stay with us or, even worse, increase over time. But with every positive step in the right direction your courage muscles get stronger. And here's another important thing to know: Excitement neutralizes fear. As you take action every success that you experience, big or small, will fuel your enthusiasm to forge ahead and accomplish even more challenging goals. With this enthusiasm in place you'll work your way through challenges with more ease. For example, if you finally decide to go back to school, you'll probably find that your excitement about learning something that's of interest to you will outweigh the heavy load of homework you were worried about handling in the beginning.

Sometimes fear is just a term we use for other obstacles. For example, sometimes fear is just a lack of fans—a network of people who believe in you and support your efforts. When my client Katie wanted to leave her job to move to a warmer climate she said that she was concerned about a couple of friends who were "realists" and made a habit of telling her why she shouldn't give up her home. Well, just about everyone has a pessimist in his or her life who will gladly inform him or her of why something won't work. When I hear this concern I see it simply as a lack of fans.

In the beginning, when you're making important life changes, you'll need to be flooded with positive support and plenty of good news. The start of any plan is the most vulnerable time, and you'll have to protect your desires by making a deliberate request to only hear positive feedback that strengthens your resolve. Certainly, if you do have close family members or friends who tend to be wet blankets, go back to chapter four and use those skills to take the necessary steps to stand up for yourself. Don't waste your time trying to convince naysayers of the viability of your plan. These folks usually get energy from conflict, and their investment in why something won't work fuels the drama.

Let me offer you a piece of advice that I received long ago:

Don't go to the hardware store for milk. Stick with people who have your best interests at heart. With the right fans in place you'll get the energy and motivation you need to change your life. Now that you have a circle of support in place this shouldn't be a problem.

Take Action! Get the Facts

Finally, you may recall that one of Victoria's action steps was to contact two travel/food writers to conduct an informational interview. This is an extremely useful step when considering any kind of life change. Traditionally used for changing jobs or exploring new career options, this type of interview will help you to get the facts behind the fear, and find the path of least resistance so you can avoid the common mistakes others have made. By gathering information from those who have already done what you'd like to do, whether it's move to another part of the country, redecorate your home, or change your job, informational interviews will help you to move forward with ease.

When you're well prepared and respectful of people's time, you'll find that most people will agree to speak with you. To be prepared I recommend that you have questions in writing before you interview someone. Here are some questions to choose from:

1. If I were to think of this change as a three-stage process, what would the three stages be?
2. What kinds of skills will I need to make this change?
3. Where should I invest my time and money first?
4. Where should I not invest my time and money?

5. If you had it all to do over again, what would you do differently? What mistakes might I avoid making?

6. What have been your major ups and downs? How might I prepare for them?

7. Is there anyone else you recommend I speak with before embarking on this journey?

When my client Sam met with someone to discuss moving cross-country he was told to be sure and visit the place at least three times before making a commitment. This information proved to be invaluable. On the first two visits he checked out the real estate market, the school system, and other practicalities, and everything fit his plan. On the third visit, however, he realized that the community he was considering had very few newcomers and therefore it would be difficult to make inroads into an established social scene.

When my client Martha interviewed an interior decorator to discuss her plans to redo her kitchen she discovered that she could save money in the long run by hiring a professional to make a preliminary plan. An informational interview I recently conducted saved me several thousand dollars when I discovered that an action I was about to take to support my business was unnecessary.

Once you've completed your informational interviews you now have a wealth of information to consider. Using your journal, sit down and ask yourself a few questions. Questions like:

1. How do I feel about the information I received? Do I still want to move forward or do I have any reservations?

2. How do I need to prepare emotionally? Physically?

3. Based on what I've learned so far, is there a different area or direction I might want to consider?

4. Do I need to speak with someone else? If so, whom?

As you conduct your informational interviews, be sure to have a separate sheet of paper dedicated to further actions you may need to take. You'll be adding these steps to your action plan. This will help when it comes time to act.

Once you've created your action plan, anticipated and handled any obstacles, and gathered the appropriate information you might need, it's time to move forward.

Take Action! Get Moving!

Your values are clear. You've got your action steps in place. You've identified any potential obstacles and revised your plan. The next step is easy: Get MOVING! First, create an "Action Area" using the format below in your journal. You'll use this area to keep track of your progress. Next, copy your action plan into this section. Then, as you consider each item, put a "by when" date next to it and be sure to share this date with your partner or group. Remember that accountability and deadlines are your friends.

Write your action plan like this:

Actions	By when	Additional Info/Actions	Date Completed
1. _____			
2. _____			
3. _____			

4. _____

5. _____

As you act on these items, check them off or write any additional information you've learned that will set you up for the next action step. For example, if you'd like to find a relationship and you get information on a great singles event, write the details in the action area of your journal and update your action plan. Your new plan may include a combination of items from your brainstorming session, action ideas from your informational interviews, or the results of what you've learned so far. With this information you're ready to create your next five action steps so you can begin to act again.

This process isn't rocket science. Once we figure out what needs to be done it's doing it that's usually the problem. The idea is to build in a routine or regular habit of reassessing your actions and updating your plan. To do this I recommend that you choose one day a week when you'll sit down, turn to the action area of your journal, and review the week's results. There should always be time scheduled in your calendar for this kind of assessment. Plus, one of the best benefits of doing this is seeing the fruits of your labor. By checking off items and monitoring your progress you'll keep yourself motivated to stay in action.

Make a commitment to do at least one action per week. If your schedule is busy, don't let a lack of time stop you! Break down one step into smaller steps. For example, if you don't have time to take a class on interior design, buy a book and begin studying on your own. The point is to do whatever you can to move forward in centering your life around your values.

When you decide to make life changes there is always a certain amount of fear and reservation. Will I succeed? Are these really the changes I need to make? Will I regret my choices once I've made them? These types of questions represent the normal self-doubt that occurs whenever we decide to take action to honor our values. Use your partner or support group to guide you through these murky waters. Remember that once you start acting the excitement and enthusiasm you feel will neutralize your fear and keep you motivated.

Just a few other reminders: When you get stuck it's a signal that you need to open your mouth and ask for help. Make this a habit. Default to asking for guidance the moment you notice that the action area of your journal is collecting dust. Any obstacle can be overcome with the support of others. Also, expect to make mistakes—lots of them. This is a lifelong process of growing and evolving over time. Be gentle with yourself. Whenever we embark on a journey it's expected that we'll veer off course at given times throughout the process. Let these mistakes guide you to your next step.

Finally, when you begin to orient your life around your values, you engage Divine support. It's as if you step into right alignment with the universe and doors start to open. I remember a stunning example of this while working on one of the "Lifestyle Makeover" shows. I worked with a woman I'll call Paula who had a dream of starting her own cooking business. Paula said she was having trouble getting started because she needed a commercial kitchen with enough space to cook large quantities of food. After participating in a brainstorming session Paula was given the suggestion to look for a commercial kitchen that she might borrow, maybe at a restaurant or community center nearby. Paula decided to visit her local community park service—a place where they held summer camp for kids. Once inside she noticed a large commercial kitchen and, thinking that the chances were slim to none, asked about it anyway.

Not only did the park service say that Paula could use their kitchen, she could use it for free in return for teaching one cooking class. They even offered to let her students help her cook as part of the curriculum! Paula left there in shock. With no more excuses, she was ready to roll.

There are clues everywhere. You just need to pay attention—a hunch to call a certain person, a surprise suggestion from a brainstorming participant, or a great idea that you stumble upon in a magazine. Act on these clues. They are simply the Divine opening doors to your next step!

RESOURCES

Books

Think and Grow Rich by Napoleon Hill (Mass Market Paperback, 1990)
This classic book will change your life.

Websites

www.monster.com
A comprehensive site offering great career guidance and opportunities.

www.freeagent.com
This website provides a business-to-business, e-commerce platform that enables buyers of project-based resources to connect with freelancers and consultants in various fields of expertise.

www.alexander-everett.com
Alexander Everett is a wise and loving teacher whose books and tapes will help you to center yourself in order to make wise choices for your life.

CHAPTER EIGHT

Create a Larger Vision
for Your Life

L
EADING A LIFE OF MEANING AND PURPOSE ultimately creates the desire and ability to make a larger
contribution. If there's one thing I've learned over the
last ten years, it's that nothing can top the deeply satisfying experience of using your unique gifts to improve the world in
some meaningful way. Whether it's helping to end world
hunger, raising a child to be an adult with a strong sense of integrity and character, or treating everyone you meet with dignity and grace, the role you play in making the world a better
place is significant.

Now, more than ever, most of us realize that we are each a
part of a global community. Each one of us has a responsibility
to stay conscious of this global connection so that we may
honor the dignity of all human beings. As you've already
learned by taking part in this program, the most powerful way
to make a difference in the world is to first make a difference in
your own life. By doing the work outlined in this book, you've
developed the courage, confidence, and character you'll need to
not only lead a life that honors your values, but one that makes a
positive difference in the world. You have set in motion the un-

folding of your Divine assignment. Now you're ready for the most important step.

Ten years ago my first coach asked me a question that motivated me to think beyond my individual goals toward how I might create a larger vision for my life. He said, "Cheryl, as you consider your values and the work you'd like to do in the world, what do you want for people?" My response was immediate, "I want people to know that they have a choice about how they live their lives."

Upon hearing this answer, he challenged me to be more specific. "What do people need in order to know that they have choices?" he asked. "Well," I replied, "They need to feel empowered. I want people to feel empowered to make choices that will allow them to live the lives they most want to live."

Once I knew what I wanted for others, and what others needed in order to make choices in their lives, I was ready to look at how I might be of service. What could I provide that would help people to feel empowered enough to make changes that would improve the quality of their lives? This part was easy. I had always been a big believer in providing simple, practical tools that helped people to make manageable changes with joy and ease. With this in mind, I created a vision statement that continues to guide my work today:

"I want people to have the practical tools and resources they need to lead high quality, authentic lives."

When you create a larger vision for your life you consciously make a decision to think beyond yourself. You become less concerned with individual gain and more concerned with how others will benefit from your actions. This does not mean that you become selfless or that your needs no longer matter.

On the contrary, it's imperative that you take good care of yourself so that your giving comes from a pure place—a healthy place without attachment to what you'll get in return. This is when service becomes a sacred experience.

When you make a choice to be of service to others, you gain the courage and sense of determination that will fuel your efforts. With a solid vision in place, you also become less concerned with your individual fear or self-doubt and more committed to taking the actions that will support your larger vision. For example, when my client Rich lost his brother to a drug overdose, he was faced with overcoming one of his greatest fears. A shy and introverted young man, Rich was devastated. Several months after his brother's death, he was asked to give a speech to the student body of his local high school about the experience of losing his brother and on the dangers of using drugs. Although Rich had an enormous fear of public speaking, he was more concerned with helping other families avoid the tragedy that his family had faced. His larger vision allowed him to put his fear aside.

Take Action! Create Your Larger Vision

To create a larger vision for your life, you need to identify how *you* would most want to improve the quality of life for others. If you could give the people of the world a gift, what would you give them? If you could heal the world of some malady, what would you heal? If you could contribute to others in your community what would that contribution be? What do you want for others?

When considering the following questions, take your time and be specific. Use your journal to explore and record your answers.

1. What do I want for people?
2. What do they need in order to have this?
3. How will I support them in fulfilling this need?

As you consider this last question, keep your four essential values in mind. How might you use one or more of your essential values to serve your vision? When you align your values with your method of contribution you create a powerful force for good.

Once you've worked through the answers to the above questions, put your vision statement into one succinct sentence that feels direct and powerful. Write your larger vision here:

What I want for people is

_____

Your vision may shift a bit over time. Don't be afraid to go back and refine it as needed. Then, create a powerful and personally meaningful visual reminder of this statement. You might create a large colorful sign or a message on your computer's screen-saver. As simple as this may seem, this vision will help create miracles in your life and in the lives of others.

When you make a decision to invest in your inner development, you engage a Divine power to support your efforts. This same force will open doors for you as you set out to serve the vision you've created for your life. Once you're clear about what you want for others, and you begin taking the actions to make it happen, it's as if you've stepped into a flowing river that gently takes you where you're meant to go. My friend Andrew knows exactly what this is like. Listen to his story.

In 1989 Andrew Carroll was struggling to make it through his first year of college. He had big plans for his life. He wanted to earn an English degree and head to Los Angeles to become a film producer. His primary goal was clear—Andrew wanted to make money—lots of it.

Just before Christmas of that same year, while preparing to take his final exams, his dad called with some disturbing news: his family home in Washington, D.C., had been completely destroyed by fire. Everything his family owned was gone.

When Andrew received the news, he was surprised to find that after years of hoarding material possessions like CDs, clothes, and books, the one thing that caused him the most pain was the loss of the letters he had saved throughout the years from his family and friends. They were irreplaceable.

Andrew's personal experience of losing his home sent him on a spiritual journey that opened his heart. He began to seriously reevaluate his life. How important was the pursuit of money? Was he spending enough time with family members and friends? How would his career ambitions make a difference in the lives of others?

Once he returned to school, Andrew felt drawn to volunteer at a local homeless shelter. While there, he started an initiative called "A Better Christmas Project" and papered his community with requests for donations of toys, books, and other items for homeless families. The members of his community rose to the occasion and donated far more than Andrew ever imagined. Remembering this event he said: "As the donations came in, I was overwhelmed by the generosity of people. It was the most extraordinary feeling to be able to rally people together to help others in need." Seeing how easy it was to make such a big difference in people's lives, Andrew stopped to consider how he might combine his *values* with his *vision*.

Fueled by the loss of his letters, Andrew embarked on a journey to educate others about the value of connecting with loved ones through letter writing. He launched the "Legacy Project" with the idea of collecting historically significant letters and sharing them with others. After his request for letters appeared in a "Dear Abby" column, Andrew received over 50,000 responses!

Andrew's next step would become an enormous labor of love. Most of the letters he received were written during wartime. Over the next three years, he gathered the most touching of them from all over the world with the intention of sharing them in a book. Deeply moved by these vivid accounts, he wanted to give readers a first-hand experience of the life-changing effects of war. And he wanted to show how letters heal, inspire, offer hope, and express love.

In May of 2001 he published some of the most inspiring of these letters in a book called *War Letters,* donating every penny of his significant book advance and royalties to non-profit groups that support peace efforts and veterans' organizations around the world.

When I asked Andrew about how his personal journey grew into a global crusade, he offered the following: "What started out as a desire to help my community turned into a much larger vision: an international campaign to educate others about the importance of staying connected through letter writing. I never had a 'grand plan.' It was amazing. The harder I worked, the more doors opened to bring my message to the world. By staying committed to my larger vision and engaging in work that was spiritually and emotionally rewarding, the project took on a life of its own and everything fell into place."

Andrew's book not only went on to be a New York Times Bestseller, but a PBS documentary too. At the time of this writing, the audio book version of *War Letters* has even been nominated for a Grammy. And, while Andrew thought he'd left his film career behind, the Universe had a different plan. Andrew is currently working with the highly acclaimed Sundance Institute Theater Program on a dramatic performance based on his book.

Andrew's values of "community" and "family" have changed the lives of many. Not only has his work contributed to veterans and families affected by war, it touches us all by underscoring the strength of the human spirit to live through the worst, most inconceivable circumstances. You can learn more about the Legacy Project (and how you can contribute your letters) by visiting his website at: *www.warletters.com*

PUT YOUR VISION INTO ACTION

Once you've identified your vision, it's time to put your heart and soul behind it by aligning it with your values and developing an action plan. You don't need the perfect plan or a groundbreaking idea, you just need to take action. To do this, pick a project—a values-based project—that will allow you to fully express your vision. The size of the project doesn't matter. For example, my client Ashley values nature. When she created her vision statement, it looked like this:

"I want people to live in a clean and healthy world."

To fulfill her vision, Ashley created a simple project: Every morning, as she takes her daily walk, she takes a bag with her so she can pick up any stray garbage along the way. She calls this project "Operation Clean Up," and uses it as her way of contributing to a cleaner environment. Her friends are aware of this project and when they join her on these walks, they're required to bring a bag too!

Take Action! Create a Values-Based Project

As you review your vision statement consider the actions you'd like to take to fulfill your vision. If you're not sure what to do, ask your partner or Life Makeover Group for help with ideas. Share your vision statement and your essential values with the group. You might even hold a brainstorming session to get a variety of ideas.

Here's how to get started:

1. Decide on a project.

2. Give your project a name.

3. Use the three-step process from chapter seven on page 201 to create a plan for action. The three steps are:
   • Brainstorm your way to a plan of action
   • Anticipate and handle any obstacles
   • Act

Start with small steps. Don't worry about doing things perfectly, just focus on taking action. To help inspire you, let's look at some examples of people who are making a difference in the world by putting their values to good use.

Lorraine White grew up without positive role models in her life. Raised in a stressful environment, Lorraine struggled through her childhood and adolescent years. At age thirty she sought the help of a good therapist when her marriage hit a crossroad. The experience was a powerful one. The therapist became a loving mirror who reflected back Lorraine's greatest qualities and gifts. As a result of this life-changing experience, Lorraine was inspired to provide the same kind of support to others. Her idea was simple: rather than wait until the adult years to get the positive role modeling we all need, why not provide it to children at a much earlier age.

Reflecting her highest value of "love," Lorraine started "Future Possibilities," a nonprofit organization that provides coaching and after-school programs for children. There are more than 300 coaches who work with children one-on-one to help them develop the confidence and self-respect they need to enter adulthood with a solid character in place. Over the last eight years, more than 250 companies have joined with Future Possibilities to provide character education programs and life skills to children throughout the United States and Canada. As of this writing, her organization is now expanding its reach worldwide. You can learn more about Future Possibilities by visiting *www.futurepossibilities.org.*

While Lorraine's project is going global, Kevin's is focused on his hometown. He's found a simple way to share his value of beauty with others. Kevin loves to garden and each year he grows hundreds of tulips in his yard. During the blooming season, Kevin visits his garden every afternoon, cuts fresh tulips and offers them as gifts to those who pass by his home. Once cut, he spreads them out on top of the hedges that surround the perimeter of his yard and invites people to take as many as they'd like. These tulips are his way of adding beauty to the lives of others.

Alan Clements has found a creative way to express his value

of freedom. In the early seventies, Alan gave up a full scholarship to study law at the University of Virginia and enrolled in the first American Buddhist University in Boulder, Colorado. He went on to spend almost ten years in Burma studying meditation and eventually became a Buddhist monk. Forced to leave his spiritual family behind by the military dictatorship, what began as a personal search for freedom turned into a campaign for justice.

Alan set out to bring Burma's nonviolent struggle for freedom to the attention of others by publishing several books including *The Voice of Hope* with Aung San Suu Kyi—Burma's Nobel Laureate and elected leader for their democracy movement. Since then, his support of Burma has blossomed into an international campaign for human rights. Alan has found a new way to share his message of freedom and hope with the world—a one-man show called "Spiritually Incorrect." Filled with personal stories and his perspective on life, his improvisational performance is a call to action. He challenges his audiences to bring more compassion and love to the world. You can learn more about his work by visiting: *www.worlddharma.com*.

Whether you decide to run for political office, implement a recycling program in your community, visit a nursing home and read to the elderly, or start a foundation, your contribution is important. Get started on your project today!

SUPPORT THE SUCCESS OF OTHERS

There is another way that you can serve the greater good of humanity with the skills you've learned: support the success of others. Now that you've become aware of how important it is to express your power and protect your dreams, doing the same for others is an important next step. For example, you might gently challenge loved ones to stop hiding their power or inspire a family member to pursue an important dream. You might even play the "Face Your Fear" game with a friend who needs to build his or her courage muscles.

Here are some other things you can do:

- Offer your help. Support the dreams and goals of others by offering to participate in a brainstorming session or by providing helpful resources.

- Look for what works. When a friend, family member, or colleague has the courage to share a dream or desire, underscore the strengths of their plan and the qualities they possess that will allow them to make it a reality. Refrain from sharing any criticism or negativity. Shine a light on what works instead of citing potential blocks.

- Eliminate sarcasm and teasing from your vocabulary. Learn to look for and acknowledge the strengths and talents in others.

- Be a Big Brother or Big Sister.

- Refuse to participate in gossip of any kind.

- Shift your conversations from suffering to success. For example, when visiting with friends, talk about what's working in your life and encourage others to do the same.

- Start a Life Makeover Group.

- Mentor an up-and-coming colleague.

- Serve as a guide for a teen or college student as they follow the program outlined in this book.

I still remember Helen Chen, the woman who evaluated my first speech at Toastmasters almost fifteen years ago. And I remember her for a reason—she was a positive, powerful influence in my life. *You* can have that kind of influence on someone's life too. Now that you know that everything you say and do could have an enormous positive impact on the future of someone close to you, how will you behave differently?

Take Action! Lift a Spirit

Make a conscious decision to support one person. Choose that person and write his or her name here:

_____

Next, how will you support this person? List three examples of what you can do here, and put a date by when you will do each one. Also, put a reminder on your calendar!

       1. _____

       2. _____

       3. _____

Spend a little extra time with a coworker who could use your help on a difficult project. Make a point to acknowledge the strength of one family member or friend everyday. You might simply become a friendly face for an elderly neighbor who lives alone by dropping in to say hello, or by doing a few chores like changing a lightbulb or picking something up at the grocery store. While I know that most of us have busy lives, let's not forget what really matters—our connection to one another.

In addition to supporting the success and well-being of one

another, the most important way to create a future where every human being is able to fulfill their greatest potential is to invest in the personal and spiritual development of our children. By using these skills to influence the lives of younger generations we will move toward creating a more peaceful and sustainable world. Let's look at some of the practical ways in which we can all make a difference in the lives of children.

EMPOWERING OUR CHILDREN

One of the most significant contributions we can make to the world is to empower our children to lead their own lives. You can do this by modeling the skills that you've learned throughout this program, and by offering guidance that will build a young person's confidence and self-esteem.

Whether you are a parent, aunt, uncle, teacher, or grandparent, increase your awareness of the rules that you reinforce. You can start with the rules I referred to in the introduction. To refresh your memory, they are:

Stop apologizing when you've done nothing wrong.

Be courageous.

Think big.

Be ambitious.

Don't be modest.

Be seen *and* heard.

Be enthusiastic.

Be proud of who you are and what you know.

Keep your expectations high.

Go for it!

Each day we have an opportunity in small ways to encourage these new rules. My sister Donna reinforces the rules "Don't be modest" and "Be enthusiastic" with her two boys, Tommy and John. At our family Christmas gathering, Donna proudly announced that Tommy had made the honor roll at school. When he blushed with embarrassment and tried to hide, Donna encouraged him to stand tall and take in the accolades. She reminded him that he had worked too hard to brush off this significant accomplishment.

Consider the new rules that you'll reinforce with the children in your life. If you're a parent, you might want to discuss these rules with your entire family so together you can create a way to integrate them into your lives. If you're not a parent, make a special effort to support the mothers and fathers in your life who dedicate their time and energy to the most sacred career of all. Now more than ever, parents struggle to raise their children in a world where you can no longer ride a bike alone, and where thousands of kids play hooky every day to avoid being teased or harassed at school. Most parents work countless hours trying to support and encourage their children in spite of the challenges and influences of schoolmates, television, and society. As I watch men and women dedicate their lives to raising healthy kids, I am humbled by their commitment. As I've learned from my sisters and brothers, there is nothing more challenging or rewarding than raising a child.

Parenting in and of itself has an inherent larger vision. For example, my sister Michelle sees her job as a mom to be the highest form of contribution. From an early age Michelle was clear about her mission in life—she wanted to raise a family. After leaving high school, she went on to study early childhood development, fell in love and got married. She and her husband

Create a Larger Vision for Your Life • 235

Mark now have three small children. Michelle is passionate about being a mother.

During a conversation with Michelle about her larger vision, she said, "I am committed to raising three children who lead their lives with courage and integrity. I want them to be confident and secure in who they are, and I want others to know that they can be trusted because they are always true to their word. My job is to protect their little spirits and encourage them to view life through their own eyes instead of the eyes of others. If I can do that, I am confident that I will bring three deeply loving and compassionate adults into the world."

When I asked Michelle to name the one most important thing she needed to do to honor her vision, she said: "When I became a parent, all of my shortcomings and unresolved issues came to the surface. In order to be the best parent I could be, I chose to deal with them. I'm clear that the most powerful contribution I can make to my children is to stay committed to my own healing work. As I do, I become more aware of the healthy behaviors and beliefs that I want to pass on to them."

After talking with several parents, I'd like to offer some ways in which you might influence children in a positive direction. The examples are:

- Protect a child's sensitivity and spirit (qualities that are often squelched in our society) by modeling healthy boundaries.
- Teach children self-discipline and patience by encouraging them to stop and assess their circumstances before reacting to difficult situations. This will help them to become aware of how their actions may affect others.

- Help children to develop an on-going relationship with a power greater than themselves. Create regular daily and/or weekly rituals that bring your family's spiritual beliefs into your children's lives. For example, you might encourage them to set up a sacred place in their rooms or create their own special prayers.

- Teach children to see their mistakes as steppingstones to success. You might encourage them to become more self-accepting by developing a relationship with their own inner ally through dialogue, play-acting, or drawing.

- Teach children to trust and honor their feelings by encouraging them to tune into, and talk about, how they feel.

- Help children to develop the courage to see the world through their own eyes instead of the eyes of others. For example, one day Michelle's daughter Justine came home upset when two schoolmates made fun of her favorite dress. As a result, she had decided not to wear the dress again. Michelle asked her to close her eyes. Then, she asked Justine how *she* felt about the dress. Justine replied, "I love this dress. I think it's beautiful." With that, Michelle reminded Justine that *her* feelings about the dress were all that really mattered. Justine wore the dress again.

- Teach children about the value of contribution and service. You might encourage them to donate their toys to a local shelter or take them with you when you volunteer at a soup kitchen.

- Acknowledge their strengths. Point out a child's unique qualities regularly. You might play a game whereby you acknowledge a child's creativity, caring nature, or sense of humor once a day. By doing this you teach children to acknowledge the strengths in others too!

- Teach children to be kind to others. Do not allow teasing, negative talk about others, or physical violence of any kind.

Help them to respect and understand differences by modeling tolerant behavior.

Most important, we need to love children unconditionally—not for what they do or say—but for who they are. After all, it's their birthright.

Take just one of these suggestions and put it to good use daily. You will have a significant effect on the children in your life. Years ago, I remember having a conversation with a psychologist who specialized in working with adults who experienced childhood traumas. He pointed out that regardless of how horrible a child's upbringing might be, one encounter with a healthy adult who offered love and support could redirect the course of that child's life. I've never forgotten that conversation. You never know when you might be that person.

LEAVE YOUR LEGACY

The program outlined in this book involves an on-going process of change. The work never ends, and the rewards won't either. You will be challenged to use these skills on a whole new level with each stage of growth you experience. When you need a reminder that you have what it takes to lead your life, remember the following:

1. Know who you are. Invest in an on-going relationship with yourself by staying connected to your inner life.

2. Stop hiding your power. Let your thoughts, words, and actions express your true essence—the very best of who you are.

3. Stand up for yourself. Strengthen your relationships by telling the truth with grace and love.

4. Build your courage muscles. Look fear in the eye and use challenging situations to make you even stronger.

5. Pass up good for great. Keep your spiritual standards high so you won't undersell your needs and desires.

6. Honor your values by making choices that keep your life centered around what matters most.

7. Link your personal goals to a larger vision that enables you to truly make a difference in the world.

As you continue to use these skills you will experience the joy and deep satisfaction that comes from fulfilling your Divine assignment—the mission that allows you to express your greatest potential. Your commitment to become someone even greater than your present self will give you the courage and confidence to leave a legacy that makes this world a much better place for those who follow. Whether you're a parent who is committed to raising good-hearted children, a loving mentor to a teenager in need, or the president of a company that serves a larger community, your contribution is equally important. As you support the success of others, you'll arrive at the end of your life knowing that your presence and love made a difference. There is no greater endowment. Your ability to leave a powerful legacy rests on your commitment to this inner work— the work that will allow you to stand up for your life!

RESOURCES

Books

The Voice of Hope by Aung San Suu Kyi and Alan Clements (Seven Stories Press, 1998)
The Voice of Hope chronicles nine months' worth of Aung San Suu Kyi's conversations with British-born Alan Clements, a Burma expert and former Buddhist monk. They discuss love, truth, power, compassion, and freedom from fear as well as Aung San Suu Kyi's own brand of activist Buddhism.

War Letters: Extraordinary Correspondence from American Wars edited by Andrew Carroll (Scribner, 2001)
War Letters is a testament and tribute to the heroic contributions and astonishing literary voices of common soldiers, marines, airmen, and sailors, as well as war nurses, journalists, spies, and chaplains. It is a celebration of the enduring power and lyricism of personal letters.

The Rhythm of Compassion by Gail Straub (Tuttle, 2000)
This is a wonderful book for learning how to be of service without compromising your self-care.

101 Ways to Help Your Daughter Love Her Body by Brenda Lane Richardson and Elane Rehr (Quill, 2001)
A must read for any parent raising a daughter.

Websites

www.volunteermatch.org
This website has facilitated hundreds of thousands of connections between volunteers and organizations, providing real-world community assistance nationwide.

www.globalvolunteers.org
The next time you're planning a vacation, why not volunteer for a community project somewhere in the world and get a firsthand experience of the culture while being of service to people in need. Global Volunteers sends teams of volunteers to live and work with local people on human and economic development projects.

www.futurepossibilities.org
A nonprofit organization delivering life skills coaching programs to children worldwide.

www.worlddharma.com
The intention of this website is to bring seekers, artists, and activists together from around the world to form an open community dedicated to exploring the inseparable link between our inner journey and engagement with the outer world through creativity, freedom, and activism.

www.warletters.com
The Legacy Project's website is a national, nonprofit organization dedicated to encouraging Americans to honor and remember America's veterans through their own words by preserving wartime correspondence.

Organizations

Habitat for Humanity International
(229) 924-6935, ext. 2551 or 2552
www.habitatforhumanity.org
Join others in helping to build simple, decent, affordable houses in partnership with those in need of adequate shelter.

Big Brothers Big Sisters of America
230 N. 13th Street
Philadelphia, PA 19107
(215) 567-7000
www.bbbsa.org
Big Brothers Big Sisters of America is the nation's oldest and largest youth mentoring organization.

United Nations Children's Fund (UNICEF)
3 United Nations Plaza
New York, NY 10017
(212) 326-7000
www.unicef.org
UNICEF is mandated by the United Nations to advocate for the protection of children's rights, to help meet their basic needs, and to expand their opportunities to reach their full potential.

Volunteers of America
1660 Duke Street
Alexandria, VA 22314-3421
(800) 899-0089
www.voa.org
> Volunteers of America is a national, nonprofit, spiritually based organization that provides local human service programs and the opportunity for individual and community involvement.

The International Coach Federation
www.coachfederation.org
> The International Coach Federation (ICF) is the largest worldwide non-profit professional association of personal and business coaches that provides Professional, Master, and Internal Corporate Coach certifications. In 2001 the ICF launched a Global Pro-Bono Coaching Program. For more information on this project as well as information on finding a coach, please visit their website.

Cheryl Richardson is the author of the *New York Times* bestselling books *Take Time for Your Life* and *Life Makeovers* (Broadway Books). Her work has been covered widely in the media including *The Today Show, CBS This Morning, New York Times, Good Housekeeping,* and numerous appearances on the *Oprah Winfrey Show.* Cheryl is the co-executive producer and host of *The Life Makeover Project with Cheryl Richardson* on the Oxygen cable network.

For more information on finding a Life Makeover Group near you, or to join Cheryl's on-line community, please subscribe to her weekly newsletter by visiting her website at:

www.cherylrichardson.com